MW00784792

Lydia Richter · China, Parian & Bisque
German Dolls

A beautiful bisque porcelain head doll, which is called among collectors, especially in America, "Miss Liberty", manufactured by Alt, Beck & Gottschalck. For further description see pages 50 and 51.

Lydia Richter

China, Parian &
Bisque German Dolls

ca. 1840 - ca. 1900

Published by Hobby House Press

Hobby House Press, Inc.
Grantsville, MD 21536

Photographs: Dr. E. Ansarien: page 40, 122 (on the right), 123, 129 (middle above), 151; Alfred Barsotti: page 32, 134 (below on the left), 146; Ralph Bille: page 17 (above); Katharina Engel: page 78; Ragnhild Ericson: page 116 (above on the left); Auction House Ernst: page 17 (above); Photographer of the Museum City of New York: page 6, 96, 107, 143, 144, 145, 147, 150, 152, 153, 154, 165; Dorothy Hill: page 15 (above), 26 (lower left), 28 (above), 34 (above and middle), 35 (above and middle), 42 (upper row), 43, 46 (above on the right), 47, 48 (above on the right and below middle), 49, 50, 51, 52 (above on the right), 57, 68 (on the left), 69 (full-page), 92 (on the right), 94 (lower center), 98, 100 (both above), 120 (above on the left and middle), 124, 129 (above on the right), 138 (above on the left), 139 (above on the right), 139 (above and below on the left); Estelle Johnston: page 11, 66 (above on the left), 79 (both photos upper row), 155, 164; Klaus-Peter Jörger: page 10, 16 (middle), 17 (Below); Georg Meister: page 128, 129; Meltons Antiques: page 30, 173 (above on the left); Staff Members of the Lego Collection: page 66 (upper and medium row on the right), 92 (above and below the left), 108 (above and below middle on the left and the right), 112 (above on the left), 114 (above and below on the left, lower row 2. from on the right), 118 (whole lower row), 125, 126, 127, 129 (above on the left), 134 (above and below on the right), 136, 138 (on the right), 141 (lower row), 158 (above and below on the right), 159, 162, 163, 166, Nymphenburg: Photographs from the Bavarian Union of Arts and Crafts from 1901: page 128 (below black-and-white); Petra Prillwitz: page 14, 16 (below), 29 , 30 (above), 31 (middle), 32, 33, 46 (above and below on the left), 66 (above middle), 67 (full-page), 108 (middle and below on the right), 109, 120 (above, middle row, lower row on the right), 121, 137; Ingrid Richen: page 38 (above), 58 (above on the left),

60 (above on the left), 64 (above), 105, 156; Joachim F. Richter: page 7, 9, 12 / 13, 18, 102 / 103, 112, 113, 114, 135, 140 (above on the left); Lydia Richter: page 2, 3, 8, 9, 14 (below), 15, 16 (Fig. above), 18, 24, 25, 27, 28 (below), 29, 30 (middle), 31, 32 (5 photos), 33 (7 photos), 34 (below), 35 (below), 36, 37, 38, 39, 41, 44 (above on the right and the left, below on the right), 45, 46 (below on the right), 52 (lower row), 59, 60 (lower row), 61, 62, 63, 64, 65, 66 (all row models), 72, 73, 76, 77 81, 82, 83, 84, 85 , 86 (above and below on the right), 87, 88, 89, 90, 91, 92 (middle above, middle below), 92 (middle on the right), 93, 94 (upper row and below on the left and the right outside), 97, 99 (above on the left), 99 (above on the right), 99 (below on the left and the r ight), 100 (below), 101, 102, 103, 104, 108 (on the left), 110, 111, 113, 116 (above on the right and lower row), 117 (on the left), (above on the right and under it), 141 (above on the left and the right), 148, 149, 158 (above), 160, 161, 168 to 183; Hannelore Schenkelberger: page 25 (above and below), 114 (above middle, above on the right, below, 2. from on the left); Helgi Schweitzer: page 86 (on the left); Seeley's Oneonta New York: page 182; Strong Museum: page 68 (right picture), 70 (left picture), 71 (right picture), 74, 75, 157; H. Tichy: page 10, 16 (middle), 17 (below); Jim Via: page 68 (right picture), 70 (left picture), 71 (right picture), 74, 75, 157; Fam. Vogt: page 24, 106 (upper row on the left below).

Loan of Dolls: For the loan of some dolls for photographing for this book we thank Traudy Hähnel, who came to us as one of the first people with two trunks full of doll heads and dolls.

Laterna magica and the author would especially like to thank those persons, who helped tremendously with loans of dolls and photographs, and those with helpful support in creating this book: Dr. E. Ansarien; Margit Bandmann; Alfred Barsotti; Katharina Engel, Doll Museum Rothenburg; Ragnhild Ericson; Auction House Ernst, Mönchengladbach; Elke Gottschalk; Dorothy Hill; Estelle Johnston; Klaus-Peter Jörger, Berlin; Mr. and Mrs. Kesting, Hamburg; Virginia Langlois; Bernd Ludwig; Melton's Antiques; Dr. Mielke, Media Center Viersen; Staff Members of the Lego-Collection; Mrs. Parzinger; Meissen-Store in Munich, Maximilianstrasse; Petra Prillwitz; Evelyn Rädler; Dan Reserva; Ingrid Richen; Hannelore Schenkelberger; Fam. Schlegel; Mrs. Schmidt; Fam. Schweitzer; Kirsten Stadelhofer, Doll Museum Legoland; Fam. Vogt; Helmut Wagner, Porcellain Manufacture Nymphenburg.

Editorial cooperation:
Dr. Barbara Krafft and Gabriele Robertson.
Text on page 128: Dr. Barbara Krafft

Production: Michael T. Robertson

References:
Anka, Georgine and Gauder, Ursula:
The German Doll Industry 1815 to 1940.
Coleman, Dorothy, Elizabeth and Evelyn:
The Collector's Encyclopedia of Dolls.
Danckert, Ludwig:
Manual of European Porcelain.
Scherf, Helmut:
Thuringian Porcellain.
The quotations are taken from the book:
Collecting Pipes from Walter Morgenroth.

Illustration on page 3:
The charming profile of the "Jenny-Lind"-Doll.
Further description see page 48 (bottom left)

Translation: Michael T. Robertson

© 1993 by Verlag Laterna magica
    Joachim F. Richter, Munich,
    Federal Republic of Germany
All rights reserved

ISBN: 0-87588-411-3

Table of Contents

Shoulder head made of Parian - modelled hair style with curls and modelled blue bows with gold edges - modelled frill bordered with pearls - glass eyes - very fine painting - 6in (15 cm) high - ca. 1865 - attributed to Dornheim, Koch & Fischer - See also page 89

Introduction

To the most beautiful and fanciful china head dolls unquestionably belong those with modelled hair. These works of art were produced in the period from 1840 to the turn of the Century. Among these the lady-like china head dolls stand out above all the others as art objects rather than toy dolls. It was not so long ago, that these dolls were counted as the exclusive and true antique dolls with dealers. The finest from them are described by collectors as the aristocrats among dolls. Today they are witnesses of a large independent doll culture and overwhelm us with their diversity and creativity. Diversity and creativity betray not only the noble formed expressions on their faces but also the art of the modelled trimmings of the Meissen-Genre. Their extravagant hair styles present an out-standing time document for the hair fashion of the previous Century. One should therefore congratulate every collector, whose collection is enriched by one of these beautiful pieces.

It is even more astonishing for us to hear or to read, again and again, that before 1909 in Germany - before the appearance of the character dolls - nothing remarkable and individualistic should have been manufactured. This statement is a very prominent one that can be explained with the simple fact that these beautiful dolls are largely unknown in Germany. One should rightfully mention here, that these exquisite doll heads were in fact mainly manufactured for export. They were sent to England, France and above all to America, where they were already admired, loved and collected, while in Germany the simpler products were predominantly in trade. It is not really remarkable, that the early dolls with the modelled hair stood with the German collectors in the shadows of their more striking sisters with wigs and glass eyes, which emerged around 1880.

Even today one can still observe that the glance of most doll collectors and friends often pass rather uninterested over the heads of these dolls with modelled hair. I personally must say this was my attitude until I found a wonderful early parian doll, whose subtlety and beauty captured me immediately. From there on I searched for them when I visited a doll fair or viewed a collection.

Experts agree, that many of these early doll heads belong to the best created in this world of dolls. It is worth mentioning at this stage one man who was the largest doll expert of his time: Georg Borgfeldt. After 1880, Borgfeldt had set the task to import the best European dolls to America and to sell them there. It is certainly an indication of the beauty and quality of these early dolls with modelled hair, that he collected them privately and left them to a New York museum. Some of the most beautiful of them are presented in this book.

Because of the large quantity of picture material and the rarity of parian dolls this book originally should have been a book only on "parian dolls", which among other things documents the exquisite beauty of many here unknown pieces. However this intent soon had to be revised, after it became clear that it was unavoidable not to enter into the beginnings of china dolls. There were some doll heads manufactured out of identical molds in different types of porcelain: china, parian and later also in bisque. One cannot extract the parian dolls from this connection, without losing the complete overview about the history of the early dolls with modelled hair. Even though the emphasis of this book should lie mainly on parian dolls, the originality and beauty of china dolls is nevertheless also valued. In addition it

A full view of one of the most beautiful china dolls, the so-called Morning Glory, created by KPM Berlin, which is described on page 122.

turned out, that many doll heads, which seemed at first glance to be made from parian, were in fact at closer inspection made from bisque. Since they present to some extent the further development of parian dolls, they were by no means to be excluded from this research book.

Even though the other published doll books by Laterna magica were extremely difficult and work intensive projects, this has been our most challenging and expensive projects.* It took a great deal of work alone to procure suitable illustrative material but now that it has been completed, we are happy to share with you so many wonderful dolls. Our hope is that those unfamiliar with these dolls will experience the captivity of their beauty and again return to the world of doll collecting.

* Editor's note: Since the publication of this book, the books on antiques and collectibles by Laterna magica were sold to the publishing firm, Weltbild.

The Parian-doll from page 6 in a very charming dress.
For further descriptions see pages 88, 89.

The Beginning of the Porcelain Doll Industry

In general the interest of our readers is naturally towards their favorite dolls and less the porcelain industry, however many want to know, who manufactured the early unmarked doll heads and where and when this happened. Thus we are now already in the middle of the topic, because the very early glazed china heads and some of the parian heads were mostly manufactured in unknown porcelain factories and not in the later, largely known porcelain factories of the doll industry. Since the modellers and painters at the very start took over the famous Meissen doll heads and also the wonderful Meissen figures as models for their own work, it is necessary, to enter into the generally interesting topic of the beginnings of the porcelain industry.

Charming Figurine from KPM Meissen. These porcelain figurines were initially models for many doll heads, which were often equally decorated with hand modelled and garnished flowers.

It is said, that around 1300 Marco Polo had brought the first porcelain from China to Europe from his world travels. There the china had existed since 7th Century, but the manufacturing process (known in Europe as Arkanum) had remained for centuries a secret, since the betrayal of this secret meant in China the death penalty. The chinese porcelain arrived first of all at the courts of the princes and kings, where it provoked supreme rapture, admiration and envy. One considered the porcelain as being a wonderful and precious material with outstanding, incomparable characteristics: light, delicate, transparent and almost as thin as paper. Nevertheless it is with extreme care almost imperishable and excellently suited for the most beautiful and finest ornamental objects, a delight for all eyes. From this time on, the recipe of this "white gold" was feverishly sought after.

How Arkanum was finally discovered after centuries of searching, is described in an amusing way by a contemporary:
"Among the Europeans a German, Johann Friedrich Bötticher, from Schleiz in Vogtlande, invented the art of making porcelain. He had learned in Berlin at a druggist the "druggist trade", and in the year 1700 he had escaped from here to Saxony, because it was gossiped, that he was able to make gold. There he was held to invent a special powder for the refinement of metals, of which he had inherited some small quantity from some unknown person; but due to embarrassment he invented instead the art of producing porcelain,which had become far more important for Saxony, than the art, which one had to look for. ...The first porcelain was produced in the years 1706 on the so-called "Jungfer" (english: Virgin) in Dresden and was of brown color..." (J. Beckmann, 1777).

Three years later the porcelain was already of pure white, and on the 23rd of January 1710, the Royal Porcelain Manufacture (Königliche Porzellanmanufaktur (KPM)) in Meissen (Saxony) was founded under King August the Strong. Forty years later nearly fourteen well-known porcelain manufacturers existed in Europe. Only the finest products including dishes and ornamental objects of supreme quality were produced from this very precious material.

Meissen developed in a few decades to one of the most outstanding porcelain manufacturers of the world. This was mainly because of the King. August the Strong loved to decorate his palaces with precious porcelain and brought many important artists - modellers and painters - to his court in Dresden. Among these two stand out in particular: Johann Joachim Kändler, a genius in the creation of life-like porcelain figures and one of the most famous ceramic artists; and likewise the well-endowed painter Johann Gregor Höroldt, who enriched the palette of porcelain colors with many in between tones as well as introduced the decor of the "German flower". Kändler decisively influenced the entire European porcelain plastic art, while Höroldts controlled the influence on almost all porcelain manufactures of Europe.

Although Meissen would have gladly protected the secret of the porcelain manufacture for itself, the news of Arkanum, despite the threat of the death penalty, soon reached the cities of Vienna, Höchst, Fürstenberg, Berlin and many other European cities due to a loose tongue. This came about through the Arkanist Ringler. J. Beckmann describes this as follows:

"How to explain, that the porcelain Arkanum was found in the workers hands in such a short time, must be told, because our Ringler was a great friend of wine. The workers served him so much wine, that he soon fell into a deep sleep. Hardly had he laid down on the bench in the tavern, when the workers found his papers, which he usually carried around with him in his pockets, and each copied them to hearts content".

Amazingly Arkanum remained a total secret to the neighboring State of Thuringia until 1760, although everyone was eagerly looking for the formula. It is only correct to mention the names of the men, who have acquired independently of each other the merit for inventing porcelain for Thuringia for the third time. They were Georg Heinrich Macheleid, Johann Wolfgang Hamman and the cousins Gottfried and Gotthelf Greiner. Naturally they benefitted from the experiences of existing glass and faience manufacturing. It is known, that Gotthelf Greiner could use the knowledge from Dümler, the founder of the Coburger Fayence factory. Despite these experiences, it was in dire need of large self initiative and personal employment up to self discipline, to reach this large goal. Around 1760 it was finally so far along, that the first porcelain manufacturing factory could be founded in Thuringia. This includes the porcelain factory of Wallendorf under Gotthelf and Gottfried Greiner, which is known as the cradle of Thuringian porcelain industry, and the porcelain factory "Älteste Rudolstadt/ Volkstedt" under Georg Heinrich Macheleid.

An extremely rare, delicate shoulder head doll, whose head was made from glazed china by KPM Meissen around 1850.

Since there was no large expense for machines and capital, other numerous porcelain factories were able to be established, mainly smaller to medium family type businesses. All persons of the period were very enthusiastic of this wonderful white porcelain, and the company founders were expecting to become wealthy, rather quickly.

Porcelain manufacturers, established in Saxony and Prussia, were appointed to supply the princes and kings with porcelain goods. Those factories found in Thuringian were mainly based on private initiative and carried their own risk. Thus they had to find their own markets outside of the royal courts. These markets would consist of the wealthier class for whom more low-priced products like dishware, vases, pipes and other articles had to be produced.

From the 18th Century there is no information concerning the manufacture of doll heads, however at the beginning of the 19th Century there is some information about small numbers of china heads appearing. So for example (according to Danckerts, Book on European Porcelain, 1973) in New York a glazed pink painted porcelain doll head with a sword marking made by KPM Meissen from the period before 1825, was auctioned. A mass production however - as far as its known - was first started around 1840.

About 1860, the toy manufacturers attention was drawn towards the porcelain doll heads. The beauty of the doll heads made from this precious porcelain struck them. Beside the still quite young porcelain industry in Thuringia and the surrounding regions, there already existed from the 14th Century, an important toy industry with worldwide reputation. They produced wooden toys; wax, paper-maché and wooden dolls, as well as doll heads and doll bodies. Owing to rich raw materials, good means of transport (state roads) and cheap labour, this region was ideal for a large toy industry. It was only logical therefore, that the interested toy manufacturers soon bought porcelain doll heads from the porcelain manufactures and took these into their assortment. Some of these manufacturers produced their own doll bodies, others bought these components from different suppliers and assembled the dolls together ready for sale.

After success was apparent, different companies, both porcelain as well as toy manufacturers, began to concentrate their program more and more towards porcelain doll heads and parts, bathing dolls and other porcelain toys. Of course many of the early porcelain manufactures, such as KPM Meissen and Berlin, who had tried to produce the first glazed porcelain heads, soon shut down this side of production. Others however, such as Alt, Beck & Gottschalk, Kling & Co. and Simon & Halbig, went mainly over to producing these type of doll heads. Again others, like the toy factory J.D. Kestner in 1860, bought up porcelain factories and specialized likewise on the production of doll heads made from porcelain.

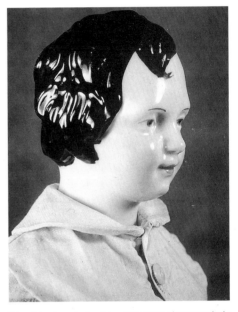

From the old Thuringian toy manufacture and the new art of porcelain manufacture developed around 1860 the beginning of the porcelain doll industry. In Thuringia porcelain makers, arcanists, sculptors and modellers either were educated or settled there. At first Meissen was the initial example, however this changed fundamentally after 1880, as the porcelain doll industry created its own independent design methods and began to go its own way. From then on its concentration was mainly on the production of toy dolls.

Shoulder head of a boy with very characteristic features made from glazed china. He was made by KPM Berlin around 1850. The hair is modelled and painted brown, he has painted light blue eyes. The inside of the shoulder plate is marked with the red empire apple (a typical marking of KPM). He is 17in (43 cm) large.

Simultaneously with Germany, from 1840 onwards, glazed porcelain heads were also manufactured in the neighboring countries, e.g. in Sèvres and Jacob Petit, Fontainebleau in France, Lippert & Haas, Schlaggenwald in Bohemia, Royal Copenhagen in Denmark and Rörstrand, Lidköping in Sweden. Indeed the share of the entire porcelain doll manufacturing was not large in those foreign countries at that period.

From the artistic porcelain figure to the toy doll

A small figurine with modelled on bonnet, which is similarly found quite often on doll heads. Produced by KPM Meissen.

Until today it was not definite who in Europe was the first to manufacture porcelain doll heads. However it was known, that the Royal Porcelain Manufacture Meissen belonged to the earliest producers. It is worth mentioning here once more the Meissen doll head from 1825 shown by Danckert. At that time such doll heads were only test models and were only produced as byproducts. The Meissen assortment included mainly luxurious dishware and some extravagant artistic porcelain. An example of this is the figurines in wonderful costumes (Rokokofigurines) - so precious, that they were preserved in display cases and could only be bought by the courts and the wealthy upper class.

From the porcelain figure to the porcelain bust and from there to the porcelain doll head was really no long step; the idea only had to be born. The ideas of Max Adolf Pfeiffer could have lead towards this. As the director of the Meissen factory, Pfeiffer is quoted as saying "that one should entrust the porcelain figure with a task, which will lead it out from the isolation of the display case".

Around 1840 the first porcelain doll heads were produced commercially. Besides the KPM Meissen, KPM Berlin also belonged to the earliest and best manufacturers, and shortly there after smaller porcelain manufactures began to produce these heads as byproducts, even though mostly in a simpler form. Since Meissen already enjoyed large respect because of the high standard of its products, it was not astonishing, that many modellers and painters of different manufactures conformed initially towards these outstanding models. Meissen produced above all, heads with elegant lady faces, which differed far more clearly from the later usual cute doll faces, and many other manufactures produced these likewise. Inspirations however were taken from the beautiful Meissen figurines and artists began to decorate the porcelain doll heads with modelled flowers, bows, hoods and bonnets. Sometimes such heads did not only have cast on trimmings but also trimmings that were produced by hand. For example frills and flowers, which were frequently known in America either as "Meissen or Dresden decorations" because of their stylistic art. Meissen because the Royal Porcelain Manufacture was resident there, and probably Dresden, because many artists, modellers and painters lived there, who worked for Meissen.

These dolls can not yet be called proper toy dolls, for the simple fact that they were not suitable for childrens hands. However older girls could play with them and possibly produce their own clothes for them. Basically these decorated dolls were more of an ornamental porcelain, that adorned the home and pleased the eye. This fact did not exclude however, that small children were given these artistic dolls as presents. This did not happen frequently and then only on certain festive occasions (such as baptism and birthdays). Subsequently the precious doll (like jewelery) was kepted safe, until the child had attained the right age and the necessary maturity. These dolls were either placed in display cases or packed into a chest, where they remained for many years.

Naturally the children's wish for proper toy dolls did not remain unconsidered. Around 1850 bathing dolls and from 1860 Nanking dolls were produced, which one can mark as being toy dolls. Old catalogs not only show porcelain heads with lady-like faces but also some with child-like expressions and short hair. Even male doll heads, according to catalogs, were being sold between 1845 and 1865. Child-like doll heads are very rare today. This is mainly due to the fact that very few children were proud owners of a porcelain head doll but expensive cost and fragility add to the rareness. The male doll heads are rare, because they were never in demand, therefore produced only in limited editions.

There exists however no doubt, that the porcelain doll heads despite their fragility and although there were other successful doll materials like wax, wood or papermachè, became a great success. Nevertheless wishes for improvements emerged. Already around 1850 the manufacturers were of the opinion that the porcelain heads with all of their beauty and strong glossiness seemed unnatural and were thus not perfect. So they directed their attention towards an especially fine, white, dull and transparent type of porcelain: parian, developed around 1850 in England (see page 17, parian doll heads).

The first so called parian dolls appeared around 1860 and provoked the rapture and admiration of the buyers. Those still preserved examples (several in the Meissen-Genre) show predominantly charming ladies and girl faces, the diversity of their fascinating hair styles, blouse upper parts arouse a past age again to life. One can consider them as being a document of contemporary history capturing the hair fashion of the 19th Century. The faces appear more appealing, but the parian dolls are more of an art object than a toy doll.

The parian doll heads were already manufactured to a large extent by the porcelain doll industry, while other porcelain manufactures returned back to producing their original assortment. The period of the exquisite parian dolls was quite short. It was not due to its appearance, which was unsurpassing in its beauty, but to the fact that they were not made for children's hands. In addition their white marble skin color was unnatural. One therefore started to paint the dull porcelain with a flesh-like tone, and from then on spoke not of parian, but of bisque doll heads.

It is not to be denied, that the delicate rosy shading appeared more warmer and alive, and so around 1880 fewer parian and more bisque doll heads were sold, which were still produced for a short period in the same manner and beauty as the parian dolls - namely with the fine hair styles and decorations. The hair remained still modelled, but that very soon was counted as being old fashioned. Around 1880 came the girl doll with its lovely childlike face, sleep eyes and wig. These fine dolls with sleep eyes and extravagant wigs were at first a luxury good.

In the last quarter of the 19th Century, the prices for porcelain had sunk so far, that it could be produced rather inexpensively and made more accessible to the general public. A certain mass production was established, when a large demand existed. The point in time had come, that these porcelain doll heads had found their proper use, namely for them to be taken into the arms of children and to be played with as toys. For this purpose simpler, but mainly undecorated doll heads with simple hair styles (glazed and unglazed) were produced in large numbers. Of course their quality was not the best because they had to be inexpensive, but among these one can still find a number of beautiful heads with a lot of radiance and in good condition. So these simple doll heads with modelled hair and painted eyes had a certain beauty of their own. Many collectors today still unfortunately do not have the eye for these masterpieces. It is regrettable, as these heads are also collectable.

Bathing children, also called "Frozen Charlotte", "Frozen Charly", "Pillar Dolls" or "Tea Cup dolls". They were produced by almost all porcelain factories, that also manufactured toy articles, usually they were not marked. They came onto the market around 1850 in many sizes and different types of porcelain, standing, sitting and also lying in the bathtub, with white, pink or black skin color, usually with modelled black painted hair, however also with brown or blond painted hair, rarely also with wigs, even with decorations (such as bands, bows, bonnets), usually unclothed but sometimes with modelled clothes and boots or with clothes made of material.

Around 1900 the popularity of these charming dolls with their modelled hair, which no child's hand could tousle, had sunk so far down the scale, that they were hardly manufactured anymore, besides as Nanking or as small dolls. This is the reason that experts among collectors love these early dolls and know how to enjoy their gracefulness and uniqueness.

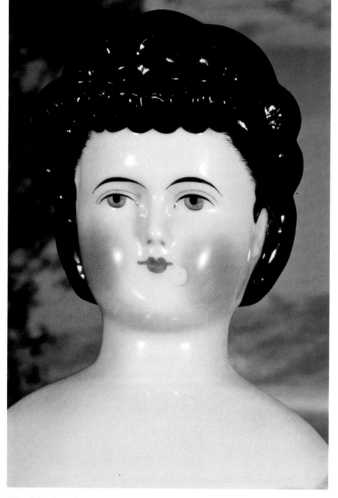

Rear view of doll pictured on the right with the well recognizable modelled bow.

Shoulder head made from china - without markings - modelled hair style - painted eyes - leather body - 22in (56 cm) large - approx. 1865 - manufactured by the company Hertel, Schwab & Co. (see page 176, the raw model above left).

The Porcelain Heads

All of the doll heads presented in this book are made of porcelain. This word has to be defined with a general meaning. In the language of the doll scene one distinguishes the following porcelains:

China porcelain: Glazed, initially mostly pink or flesh tinted, later predominantly untinted, white, on rare occasions also brown or black tinted porcelain.
The name "china", came from the origin of the porcelain from China to Europe. It has nothing to do with Chinese doll heads.
The mixture in Meissen was composed of 50% china clay, 25% quartz, 25% feldspar; in Thuringia 40 to 45% china clay, 25% quartz, 30-35% feldspar.

Parian porcelain: Unglazed, dull, untinted, white porcelain. It displays a certain similarity with the marble from the Paros island therefore receiving the name parian.

Bisque porcelain: Unglazed, dull, tinted porcelain, which resembles with its flesh tinted color that of the human skin.

Stone bisque: A somewhat minor stoneware, unglazed porcelain, whose color tends to frequently be grey. The term stone bisque is hardly used in Germany; however stone bisque is in America quite common.

Shoulder head

The liquid porcelain mass, the so called slicker, was poured with the largest portion of the doll heads into plaster molds, which is recognizable due to the smooth surface on the inside. With some of the earlier doll heads a more firm cake-like dough porcelain mass was pressed by hand into two plaster molds. The dried parts were put together again and joined using this slicker. These heads are frequently unevenly thick and uneven on the inside.

From about 1840 to around 1880, shoulder heads (head and shoulder plate in one piece) were mainly produced, sometimes with modelled breasts. The swivel breast plate head, which is essentially rarer before 1900, differs solely in that it has a narrower breast plate . The swivel head, which was mounted on a shoulder plate, also known as a swivel neck, was produced from approx. 1850 on and the ring neck head from approx. 1860. Both are very rare. Swivel heads, or revolving heads were mounted onto joint bodies made from wood, papermaché or composition, began to dominate from approx. 1880. Since early swivel heads with modelled hair on the above named joint bodies are rarely to be found, we will therefore not go into depth on these.

Swivel breastplate head

All these doll heads have a closed head crown, and as a rule have modelled hair. An exception is the early bald or round head, also called a Biedermeier head, which had no modelled hair, but often a circular place above, where the wig was secured or a slit for securing the hair (slit head).

These above named heads were manufactured in porcelain (from approx. 1840) as well as in parian (from approx. 1860 and only to approx. 1880) or in bisque (from approx. 1880). Only the swivel head, which was produced for composition bodies, was made from parian and bisque.

Swivel head

Early china shoulder head from around 1850 with fixed glass eyes and painted eyelashes.

Shoulder head made from bisque, richly decorated with night cap and shirt upper part, around 1900.

Glazed porcelain head, for further description see page 46 (on the left).

Shoulder, breast plate and swivel breast plate heads have at the lower edge of the front and back shoulder plate usually two or three, sometimes four and even five holes, but occasionally also only one hole. These holes are known as sewing holes, to which the bodies were sewn or fastened to. More rarely heads are found without sewing holes. These were either sewn or glued into the bodies, sometimes even both.

The **eyes** of the early doll heads as a rule were painted. With later heads so-called intaglio-eyes are found in rare cases. These eyes are painted, their iris and pupil were more deeply modelled. From approx. 1850 one will only find very few heads with fixed glass eyes. These glass eyes were not manufactured as a rule by the porcelain manufactures, but were bought from glass works.

The **mouth** of the early doll heads were modelled closed and painted. The so-called open-closed mouth is only to be found with later doll heads from approx. 1875. Here the lips were modelled open and painted of course, the opening between them however not cut out, so that the gap remained visible - sometimes with painted teeth (see page 161). The open mouth, which is to be found from 1890 on, had the opening cut out and teeth were placed into the opening.

Decorations: Frequently the doll heads are furnished with so-called decorations. This terminology goes back to the commonly used wording "decoration", which was used in America and today it has an international meaning, modelled trimmings on the heads of early dolls. Such trimmings can be found on the head, the neck or on the shoulder plate. For example:

Headgear: Hats, bonnets, scarfs or turbans;

Head and hair jewelry: Feathers, bows, bands, hairnets, tassles, crowns, cockades, stars, combs and even fruits, single or several flowers in different sizes, also as a crown, with or without leaves;

Neck jewelery: "Jewels" (mainly made from glass), modelled pearls or gold colored chains;

Jewelry on blouse or shirt: Frills, neckties, lace etc.; the latter could only be modelled, or tull that was dipped into slicker.

The decorations could be an element of the mold or molded on by hand after the initial mold. They are either glazed or unglazed, rich in detail or very simple, in many fine colors and also painted with gold and silver lustre. Further comparisons showed, that the more extravagant decorations were found mainly on larger heads, while the smaller ones (even if they came from the identical model), were either simplified or had no decorations at all.

Glazed porcelain heads (china heads) are well recognizable due to the strong glossiness of their glaze. At the beginning (1840 to 1870) lady faces dominated, often in classic style with long noses; long, slender necks and with many differently modelled hair styles, some already with decorations. Heads with men or childrens faces were far rarer with stocky necks and short hair styles. The rarest are swivel breast plate heads with men's faces, moustache and glass eyes. The skin color of the earlier examples were mostly soft pink or flesh tinted, otherwise predominantly white; the rosy cheeks are painted on. The earlier heads had modelled, skillful hair styles with brown, black or brown and black painted hair; about 1860 also blond hair emerged occasionally. The painting of the eyes were brown or blue, mostly with a red eyelid stroke and dotted corner of the eyes; approximately from 1850 there also were in rare cases inserted glass eyes, mostly in brown or black, with or without pupils and with or without painted eyelashes. The mouth was modelled and painted closed, the earlobes were sometimes pierced.

Different authors report, that some of the most beautiful early heads had a rosy skin color with a delicate gold lustre, which others have referred to as being nonsense. If such doll heads exist, then they must be unusually rare, for even after inquiring with numerous collectors and several museums nothing was to be learned about them, since nobody owned such a doll head.

Parian doll heads can be recognized by their dull porcelain with white skin color. The cheeks are painted in a rosy color, the mouth is usually modelled closed and painted. The eyes are still painted, usually blue, more rarely brown, often with red eyelid strokes and red dotted corner of the eyes. Inserted glass eyes are still always the exception. The hair as a rule is modelled and mainly blond, rarely brown or black painted. The earlobes are either pierced for earrings, or the earrings were modelled on immediately. Decorations are very frequently found on parian doll heads.

Parian was produced by the manufacture Stoke-on-Trent under William Copeland and used there - as far as its known - due to the high production costs only for figure-like plastics. Since however porcelain doll heads were found with Bow, Chelsea and Staffordshire markings, doll collectors were of the opinion, that they also had been manufactured there. Repeated diggings on the land of the porcelain factories did not bring any fragments of porcelain doll heads to light, so the conclusion emerged, that in England before 1900 no doll heads were manufactured from porcelain.

After 1850 the German porcelain manufacturers became aware of this dull parian. Since the formula was a secret, own attempts must have been undertaken, to acquire a similar parian porcelain. The result did not reach the fineness and transparency of the English parian. However it was more low-priced and ideal for doll heads. Besides it could be worked well and was very suitable for trimmings. Possibly this material was more like a white bisque. Thus some collectors and authors would like, that the expression "parian" be not used anymore, and that the preferred official designation be white bisque. It is a fact that around the middle of the previous century parian doll heads and dolls were advertised and that the name "parian" was used. It would not be advisable to get rid of this name - because those interested collectors in this world know that when this name is used one is talking about the early dolls with modelled hair.

Bisque doll heads with modelled hair (also called **parian-types**) from the period around 1870 to around the turn of the Century are recognized by their dull fine skin-colored tinted porcelain. This shading could fall out so fine and pale, that one could hardly distinguish, whether one was dealing with parian or bisque. That is one of the reasons, why one speaks generally of parian-type dolls and adds these light bisque doll heads with modelled hair to them. To distinguish them from another, it is advisable to hold a genuine parian head beside it and - if possible - compare the outside and inside. The skin color however can be tinted stronger in a beige or delicate pink light, which helps in the comparison. These bisque heads were produced for several years in exactly the same way as the parian heads, also with modelled hair and decorations, whereby the latter gradually became

Parian doll heads (but also china and bisque heads) with modelled hair were used also for automatic dolls, like here for the above illustrated Autoperipatetikos. It is marked: "Patented July 15th; also in Europe, 20 Dec. 1862", and has the same head like the doll on page 92 (top row in the middle). The upper body, with sewn on leather arms and stepped fingers, sits on a cardboard cone, which contains the clock work. The feet made from brass colored metal appear out of two slots from the bottom and brings the doll to move. It is wearing a silk dress, which is trimmed richly with brocade, and flows out into a crinoline, this conceals the mechanics. 11in (28 cm) large.

A beautiful shoulder head made from bisque with finely modelled hair style with a rose, as well as blouse upper part, this modelling is attributed to the company Dornheim, Koch & Fischer. approx. 1880.

Shoulder head made from stone bisque with modelled bonnet and blouse upper part, produced around 1899 for the international costume series for Butler Bros..

Shoulder head made from stone bisque with modelled pink bonnet - simple painting - cloth body - 10-1/2in (26 cm) large - approx. 1900.

rarer. Besides the blue painted eyes are glass eyes now found more frequently. The mouth is mainly closed and rarely also modelled open-closed and painted; also painted teeth are possible. From 1890 on, the open mouth with teeth became modern, which is rarely to be found with doll heads with modelled hair.

Doll heads were produced in various sizes, usually up to 12in (31cm), however also up to 25in (64cm).

Doll heads with **identical faces** were quite often produced with different hair styles and hair colors (black, brown and blond tones), with painted or more rarely with glass eyes, with or without decorations, which could fall out differently, with or without pierced ears, as shoulder heads, swivel breast plate heads or swivel heads on composition bodies (extremely rare).

The porcelain heads and parts were not manufactured by the toy factories, but by the porcelain factories.

The quality of the early doll heads produced from 1840 to approx. 1870 was excellent, this changed in the years after. Not only were fine heads of the best quality produced, but now also of lower quality. These quality differences appear not only with heads in general, but with identical heads of the same model. The different headed models were manufactured sometimes as luxury versions made from finest porcelain with detailed painting, extravagant hair style and decorations with gold lustre, but also as the cheap model with simple painting without details and with simple hair style.

These charming shoulder head dolls were produced around the turn of the century, which remind us of the cute Nippesfigures, which were reproduced china for the simple folk.

Shoulder head made from bisque with modelled night cap, collar and blouse upper part with fur edge - leather body - 20-1/2in (52 cm) large - approx. 1900.

Shoulder head made from bisque with modelled hat and bow and modelled blouse upper part - 3-1/2in (9 cm) large - approx. 1900.

Shoulder head made from stone bisque - simple painted face, nicely modelled, two colored painted bonnet with bow - 2-1/2in (6 cm) large - approx. 1900 - found in Katzhütte, presumably from Fa. Hertwig & Co.

Marking of the doll heads

Of course a decree was remitted in 1887, whereupon all doll heads that were produced for export, had to be marked with the statement "Made in Germany". A general instruction to the marking of doll heads with company names or trademarks was not given. Even though the large porcelain manufactures like KPM Meissen and KPM Berlin used their companies marking on most of their doll heads from the beginning, other numerous smaller manufactures preferred to leave their doll heads unmarked. Initially only the size numbers were burnt in and from approx. 1880 onwards mold numbers or series numbers were occasionally added. (The mold number indicated a certain type of head or face, while the series number indicated a certain edition).

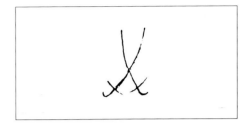
Marking KPM Meissen

Only after 1880 did some companies, e.g. Simon & Halbig and C.F. Kling & Co., mark their doll heads, so that one could identify which company they came from.

Most of the marks were either impressed or burnt in, but some were also stamped in color (blue or red, brown, green or black) or painted on by hand. They can be found on either the outside or on the inside of the front or back shoulder plate, occasionally also on both shoulder plates. With swivel heads they are impressed on the back of neck.

Marking KPM Berlin

Markings could be very different: with company names or initials, with trademarks (such as hearts, stars, circles), symbols, letters, numbers, mold or series numbers. Around 1890 it was usual to use markings, however not all companies followed this pattern. For instance the company Kestner, one of the most important producers, started to mark their doll heads only from 1910 on with their companies initials; until then they marked if at all, only with letters and numbers (Kestner Alphabet), or from approx. 1880 on with partial mold numbers. Hertel, Schwab & Co., a porcelain factory, which manufactured excellent doll heads, remained - like many others - unknown for a long time, because they hardly used a marking as a rule.

Marking C.F. Kling & Co., Ohrdruf

A special case is the jointly used clover leaf from the Greiner family used by several companies. Since the Greiner name emerges again and again in the doll history, it is worth mentioning a few facts about this diversified doll making family. The Greiners wer e originally a painter and potter family. They belong along with the Heubach family to the founders of the porcelain industry in Thuringia. Their head member Gotthelf Greiner and his cousin Gottfried Greiner as well as Georg Heinrich Macheleid and Johann Wolfgang Hamman worked around 1760 independently of each other on the reinvention of porcelain and were involved in the establishment of the Wallendorfer porcelain factory. In 1772 Gotthelf Greiner founded the porcelain factory in Limbach; 1782 the porcelain factory Grossbreitenbach and 1786 the porcelain factory Ilmenau came into his property. Five of his sons, Ernst, Johann Friedeman, Johann Georg Daniel, Johann Jakob Florentin and Johann Michael Gotthelf, acquired in 1797 the porcelain factory Kloster Veilsdorf. Johann Georg Wilhelm and Johann Andreas became in 1780 the owners of the porcelain factory Gera (a branch organization of the Volkstedter porcelain factory), Johann Friedrich, Johann Georg and Christian Daniel founded in 1783 the porcelain factory Rauenstein, and Wilhelm Heinrich was in 1799 a co-owner of the porcelain factory Volkstedt. Grossbreitenbach remained till 1869 in the property of the Greiner family. The clover leaf marking was used jointly with Limbach, Ilmenau and Kloster Veilsdorf.

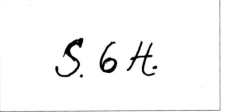
Marking Simon & Halbig, Gräfenhain

Markings, found on porcelain doll heads with modelled hair from the period between 1840-1900, and also the companies:

1000 ✕ 10

Alt, Beck & Gottschalk, Porcelain Factory, Nauendorf/Thuringia, founded in 1854, produced among other things doll heads, bathing dolls and Nanking dolls.

The company manufactured first of all household and figurative porcelain, began early (around 1860) with the production of porcelain, later parian and bisque doll heads. Only today does this become obvious when looking at the old raw models and the thereby identified doll heads, that the doll head production before 1900 was far more important than assumed and that most of these beautiful doll heads of this company were created before 1900. Above all the company specialized on portrait doll heads; so that it now seems, as if most of these same types were manufactured here. Among the known numbers of doll heads with modelled hair are: Mold numbers 772, 784, 880, 882, 890, 894 (Blue Scarf Lady, see page 57), 896, 898, 974 (long wavy hair, see page 68), 990 (with bonnet and bow, see page 69), 996 (with white shawl and purple hood, see page 71), 998 (with white bonnet, see page 70), 1000 (Highland Mary, see page 73), 1002, 1008, 1024 (with red bonnet, see page 75), 1028, 1030 (short hair), 1046 (short hair), 1054 (blue bonnet with bows, see page 74), 1056, 1064, 1086, 1142, 1210, 1214, 1218, 1222, 1226, 1254, 1288, 1304.

Markings with the initials ABG or A. B. & G., which were impressed on doll heads with wigs from approx. 1900 on, have not been found - so far known - on heads with modelled hair. Several of the companies associated dolls mentioned in this book were identified for the first time due to new knowledge found through findings of old pieces (broken doll heads, raw models and old forms), see illustrated section and pages 168 to 172.

Bähr & Pröschild, Porcelain Factory, Ohrdruf/Thuringia, founded 1871, produced among other things figurative porcelain, bathing children, Nanking dolls and doll heads. Up until now it was not however known, which of these early doll heads with modelled hair originated from this firm. Several of these I could now associate to this company (see page 173, 174).

Markings with the initials B & P, which were used from approx. 1895 on, are not known to be found on doll heads with modelled hair. The associated doll in this book was identified through an old raw model (see page 173 above on the left), further raw models on pages 173 and 174.

E B

Bischoff, Emil, Sonneberg/Thuringia, 1863-1879, Manufacturer of doll heads, which were shown in 1873 at a Viennese fair. Agents in Paris: Gottschalck & Co.

Bühl, H., & Sons, Porcelain Factory, Grossbreitenbach/Thuringia, founded approx. 1780.

Conta & Boehme, Porcelain Factory, Pössneck/Thuringia, founded 1790, produced among other things porcelain dolls, doll heads, bathing children and Nanking dolls.

D K F

Dornheim, Koch & Fischer, Porcelain Factory, Gräfenroda/Thuringia, founded 1856, produced among other things doll heads and lady heads with decorations. This company has appeared very little in the doll world until now, since most of the doll heads have no markings. Fortunately some very beautiful lady heads were found with richly modelled on flower decorations, which were marked as seen on the left. After that further heads could be identified and attributed to this company because of the similarities in the faces, modelling and pai nting (see comparisons on page 83).

Dressel, Kister & Co., Porcelain Factory, Passau/Bavaria, founded 1837. The name was changed in 1876 to A.W. Fr. Kister. While they are well known today among collectors for the charming half-dolls produced by this company, the beautiful, earlier shoulder head dolls they made are little known, and in fact quite rare.

Fürstenberg, Porcelain Factory, Lower Saxony, founded 1750, produced among other things glazed porcelain heads here.

Gera, Porcelain Factory, Thuringia, founded 1779, produced among other things doll heads (see also Greiner Family, page 19).

Goebel, William, Porcelain Factory, Oeslau/Thuringia, founded 1871, produced among other things doll heads, bathing children, porcelain children.

Gotha, Porcelain Factory, Morgenroth & Co., Thuringia, founded 1757, produced among other things doll heads.

Greiner Family see page 19.

Grossbreitenbach, Porcelain Factory, Thuringia, founded by E. von Hopfgarten 1778, 1782-1869 owned by the Greiner Family.

Hertwig & Co., Porcelain and Stoneware Factory, Katzhütte/Thuringia, founded 1864, produced among other things porcelain doll heads and bathing dolls, Nanking dolls and porcelain children.

Hertel, Schwab & Co., Porcelain Factory, pottery and ceramics, Stutzhaus/Thuringia, founded 1863, produced among other things doll heads.

According to a company paper that appeared, Hertel, Schwab & Co. was founded in 1863 and not in 1910, which had been the assumed date. However it appears as if this company was closed between 1890 and 1910.

Main production included doll heads and parts made from porcelain in different sizes, which were manufactured inexpensively, in large quantities and were exported. Many workers from the surrounding area and special workers from abroad had settled in and around Stutzhaus, found a good living here.

Like many of the other companies, who did not mark their doll heads, this company remained unknown among collectors for a long time. It is a great surprise for collectors today, that a large number of these beautiful early doll heads were produced here.

This company did not - so far known - use markings before 1910. The dolls presented in this book were associated for the first time because of findings of old pieces (doll heads and raw models), see illustrated section and pages 175 to 178.

Heubach, Kämpfe & Sontag, Porcelain Factory, Wallendorf/Thuringia, founded 1763, produced among other things figurative porcelain doll heads as well as bathing dolls.

Hutschenreuther, C.M., Porcelain Factory, Hohenberg/Bavaria, founded 1814, produced among other things doll heads and bathing children.

Ilmenau, Porcelain Factory, Thuringia, founded 1777, leased by Gotthelf Greiner in 1786, produced among other things doll heads.

Kestner, J.D., Porcelain and Toy Factory, Waltershausen/Thuringia, founded 1805. The Porcelain Factory in Ohrdruf was acquired in 1860 and produced among other things porcelain and bisque heads, Nanking dolls and bathing children. They were marked with letters and numbers (known as the Kestner Alphabet).

J.D. Kestner was the founder of the Waltershausener Doll Industry. The Kestner toy and porcelain factory belonged to the largest and most important company of this branch in Germany. It produced many of the most beautiful German

Out of a cataloque from the Kestner company.

luxury dolls. Due to worldwide export of these outstanding dolls, the Kestner company became the trademark in this area for German quality and creativity. Kestner early on advertised doll heads made from porcelain. Therefore it is practically unthinkable, that this company should not have produced doll heads made from parian and bisque with modelled hair. These have probably not been identified until recently, because no markings were available, which identified the manufacturer (see also markings of unknown manufacturers).

Kister, A.W.FR., Porcelain Manufacture, Scheibe/Alsbach, Thuringia, founded 1876 (see Dressel, Kister & Co.), produced among other things doll heads and parts, bathing children.

Kling, Christian F., & Co., Porcelain Factory, Ohrdruf/Thuringia, founded 1837, produced among other things porcelain doll heads as well as bathing children and Nanking dolls; one of the few factories, which produced besides doll heads, doll bodies.

This company also produced their most beautiful doll heads before 1900, after it had initially produced household and figurative porcelain. Among all these articles an especially beautiful face stands out, which we present in several different versions of hair styles and decorations on pages 114 to 119. Known mold numbers (before 1900): 114, 116, 122, 128 (with black comb), 129, 131, 133, 135 (with a rose in the hair), 137, 140, 141 (with flowers and leaves on the head), 142, 144 (with modelled black or brown feather), 148, 151 (with modelled blouse upper part with cords), 153, 154, 160, 161 (with flower wreath diagonally on the head and mo delled blouse upper part), 167, 170 (with modelled blouse upper part and comb on the back of the head), 182, 185 (with a braid on to p of the head), 186, 295.

Kloster Veilsdorf, Porcelain Factory, Thuringia, founded 1760 (see Greiner Family, page 19), produced porcelain and bisque doll heads, bathing children and Nanking dolls.

Kloster Vessra, Ickel, Edmund, Porcelain Factory, Themar/Thuringia, founded 1892, produced also doll heads.

Royal Bavarian Porcelain Manufacture Nymphenburg, Munich, founded 1747 by Elector Max III. Joseph. Doll heads were first manufactured from 1901.

K.P.M
Preßmarke
Seit etwa 1825
Von 1837 ab vorwiegend für
Platten und Lithophanien

KPM

Royal Porcelain Manufacture Berlin, founded 1761. At the wish of Friedrichs the Great, the merchant Johann Ernst Gotzkowski founded in 1761 a porcelain factory in Berlin, which was soon counted among the best and leading manufacturers in Europe. Between 1840-1860 among other things very beautiful doll heads were also created here (see pages 120-125, there are also further markings to be seen).

Royal Porcelain Manufacture Meissen/Saxony, founded 1710 (see pages 126, 127), the first European porcelain manufacture, produced among other things doll heads over a short period (approx. 20 to 30 years).

Limbach/Thuringia, Porcelain Factory, founded 1772 (see Greiner Family, page 19), produced among other things doll heads.

Metzler, G., & Ortloff, Gebr., Porcelain Factory, Ilmenau/Thuringia, founded 1875, produced among other things doll heads .

Orben, Knabe & Co., Porcelain Factory, Geschwenda/Thuringia, founded 1909, produced among other things porcelain heads.

Pfeffer, E., Porcelain-Faience Factory, Gotha, founded 1892, produced among other things doll heads, bathing children, and Nanking dolls.

Pohl, Gebr., Porcelain Factory, Schmiedeberg/Thuringia, founded 1871, produced among other things doll heads.

Rauenstein, Porcelain Factory, Thuringia, founded 1783 (see Greiner Family, page 19), produced among other things doll heads.

Riedeler, August, Porcelain Factory Königsee, Thuringia, founded 1872, produced among other things bathing dolls, Nanking dolls and doll heads.

Rudolstadt, Volkstedt, oldest Volkstedter Porcelain Factory, Thuringia, founded 1762 by G. H. Macheleid (see Greiner Family, page 19), produced among other things doll heads.

Schneider, Carl, heir, formerly Unger, Schneider & Hutschenreuther Porcelain Factory, Gräfenthal/Thuringia, founded 1861, produced among other things bathing children, doll heads and half dolls.

Schützmeister & Quendt, Porcelain Factory and Porcelain painting, Gotha/Thuringia, founded 1893, produced among other things doll heads and bathing children.

Simon & Halbig, Porcelain Factory, Gräfenhain/Thuringia, founded 1870, produced among other things doll heads, bathing children, Nanking dolls and small whole bisque dolls. The company belonged (besides J. D. Kestner) to the most important German porcelain factories, which distinguished itself especially through the production of the finest doll heads. They were exported worldwide, above all to America and to France.

Voigt, Gebr., Porcelain Factory, Sitzendorf/Thuringia, founded 1850, produced among other things doll heads.

Markings of an unknown manufacturer, possibly Kestner, since the company had marked their early doll heads mainly with letters and numbers (the so-called Kestner Alphabet):

5 A 5	5 H 5	4 P 9	.5 V 2
4 B 5	2 K 3	4 R 7.	4 W 0
5 B 5	3 L 5	3 S 3	5 Y 6
5 C.5.	5 M 5	5 U 2	
5 E	4 N 9		

Foreign countries

E DEPOSE B **EB**	**Barrois, E., Paris/France,** founded 1844, no porcelain factory, bought heads from other porcelain factories in France and Germany.
B & D Pat. Dec 7/10 DOTTER PAT 7/10	**Bawo & Dotter, Fischern/Bohemia,** founded 1884, since 1873 also in Limoges, according to Danckert porcelain painting in great style.
J P PAR BREVET 1317	**Petit, Jacob, Porcelain Factory,** Fontainebleau by Paris/France, founded 1790.
S	**Lippert & Haas, Schlaggenwald/Bohemia,** founded 1793, the first Porcelain Factory in Bohemia.
≋	**Royal Copenhagen, Porcelain Factory, Copenhagen/Denmark,** founded 1760.
RÖRSTRAND	**Rörstrand, Porcelain Factory, Lidköping/Sweden,** founded 1726.
Sèvres	**Sèvres (Manufacture de Sèvres), Porcelain Factory, Sèvres/France,** founded 1738.

Small doll boy, whose bisque head was marked with E.B. and was attributed to Barrois. The question arises, whether it was possibly manufactured by the company Emil Bischof.

Model Heads, Variations and Imitations

It is essential, that the collector or doll friend, who would like to identify the dolls, should also know a little about model heads. Doll heads from varying models can fall out very differently, but also can be partially remodeled, so that one can hardly recognize, from which model they came from.

A beautiful model head is the main requirement for the production of doll heads. To procure them was not always easy and often it was connected with considerable costs. Either one tried to buy an already available suitable model head or one assigned a modeler with the job of producing a new model head, be it from a living model, from a painting or out of the imagination. After all this the preparations for the necessary production to commercialize them began, which involved again considerable costs. One had to produce hundreds, even thousands of plaster molds, which were necessary for the molding of the porcelain mass. Therefore most companies owned over many years only one model head. For example it is written in a company document from the renowned company Kämmer & Reinhardt, that this company used over 25 years only one model head, nevertheless it still was the leader on the market.

Only one model head did not mean, that the identical doll head always had to be produced, for there were countless possibilities for the modeler, to remodel and to modify each possible type. It is most often difficult for even a trained eye, to recognize the original model. The expert may speak among collectors of the so-called family similarities of some doll heads, which either originated by chance or through copying. Frequently however several variations were developed from the same model head.

To create a large variety of dolls, the modeler had to come up with many good ideas. From each porcelain doll head plaster copies could be taken, which when filled out with modelling mass again produced a model head. Above all the hair colors and hair styles were frequently altered and adjusted to the respective fashion, and some heads and shoulder plates received decorations of the most abundant kind.

Also facial changes could be undertaken. One could paint the eyes small or large, insert glass eyes, or model a closed mouth first and later change it to an open-closed one or provide the open mouth with teeth. The face and nose could be broadened or narrowed, extended or shortened. The painting of the doll heads also could be changed by a rich shading. Besides such intended changes, there were also unintentional changes to the doll heads. These occurred when the porcelain shrinks by approx. 15% when fired, this changes the length and width. In addition the plaster molds were subject to strong wear and tear when casting the heads, so that the initial poured heads had still very distinctive contours like a pointed nose, while the final poured heads displayed flat contours with a round nose.

Four doll heads from the company C.F. Kling & Co., all originated from one model head, which were only remodelled respectively.

This phenomena had great influence on small doll heads, which lost through the shrinking process their individual facial expressions. Therefore the small unmarked heads with identical or similar hair styles - even if they were manufactured by different porcelain factories - can hardly be held apart, unless they have particular features.

Small simple china head, which was found on the land owned by the company Hertel, Schwab & Co..

Small doll of the type "Alice in Wonderland". Shoulder head made from parian with glazed brown hair. The painting and the similarity of the face point to the company Hertel, Schwab & Co., see illustration above.

It is long since no secret, that at that period - and like at all times - successful things were copied quickly. Besides the manufactures, who used their own model heads, there already were at the very beginning of porcelain head doll production some companies, who copied successful products from their competitors. This could be certain doll types, for example the classical beautiful lady face of KPM Meissen, or it could be the ideas coming from models, for example the portrait dolls "Alice in Wonderland" and "Highland Mary". As long as these companies made their own designs for their doll heads, the affair was relatively harmless, although the originators were surely annoyed over this. Essentially more unpleasant was the fact that some companies bought themselves the most beautiful and most successful doll heads of the competitors and manufactured from these copies and then model heads, so as to use them for their own production.

This is very noticeable when comparing old raw models and broken doll heads found in the ruins (from the time before 1900), that many doll heads of different porcelain factories are quite identical. We know of course today, that KPM Meissen was imitated quite often, however it is difficult to reconstruct which company copied from whom. One can however assume, that as a rule the smaller, poorer company, copied from the larger, financially better company, since the latter had the better specialists: sculptors, modelers and painters.

The background for this business behaviour was to be seen in the exceedingly hard competition, with the commercial existence at stake. Since a beautiful model head could be very expensive, it was the simplest method, to buy such a head and to hang on to the success of others.

Indeed one did not always copy. It is known, that smaller companies jointly used a model head, exchanged also molds or legally gave them away. Larger porcelain factories, whose capacity, just before Christmas, was not sufficient, had part of their orders produced by other companys, and again other porcelain factories delivered their white product (white raw model) to special porcelain painting companies, who then painted the heads. This might have happened either as an order from the porcelain factories or on resale cost. These painting companies quite often placed their own markings on the heads - a further circumstance, which confuses and complicates the process of finding the manufacturer.

From about 1880 on, it became usual, to place a company marking on the doll heads. Here it could become rather decieving for the buyer, especially when these business people produced rather similar markings from the better products. However the Meissen products still counted as being the best and of supreme quality, and other certain porcelain factories: Rudolstadt, Rauenstein or the A. W. FR. Kister Ltd., tried to use similar markings, whereby KPM Meissen protested furiously against this. For the prevention of the abuse of artistic property (to which also the doll faces belonged) more companies took action for legal protection. Nevertheless this behaviour of copying could not be stopped completely.

Identification of Doll Heads

Frequently the question is raised by interested collectors, whether it could be determined, who the company was that had produced these unmarked dolls.

If a doll head originated from the period before 1860, the above question must be denied in most cases, since these manufacturers do not exist any more today and also because they have not marked their doll heads. Even if one could still find documents like work sheets and work books or catalogs, it would be rather unhelpful. Under certain circumstances, these doll heads may not be illustrated in them and the descriptions may not be sufficient enough in identifying them. Also old finds (fragments, molds, heads) are useless for the doll research. If they were not found on the property of a known porcelain factory, it is not known who manufactured them.

However there is in some cases - especially for the years following 1860 - a possibility, to find the origin of many unmarked dolls. By comparing them with later identical doll heads, which have already marks, or with old molds, raw models or fragments, found either when houses are torn down or excavation work is being done on sites of old known porcelain factories.

Fortunately such old pieces could be photographed for this book, so that a large portion of the photographs published here can be used for comparisons - (for instance an unmarked doll with identical doll head or dolls, who are marked already or their producers are known), in determining the manufacturer of unmarked dolls. If the latter should be identified, it is recommended that one take the doll in one's hand and compare it with the illustrative material of this book, to find an identical or similar one. Doll heads with identical faces, hair styles or also decorations will not be to difficult and one will be quite successful at first glance. However if the faces fall out somewhat different, and the hair styles and decorations have been remodelled, this will cause some difficulties, and sometimes be even impossible.

It is of importance, to find references on doll heads that point to a common manufacturer; for even though many porcelain factories have painted and modelled partially similar or identical, most of them leave behind certain typical features.

First of all a similar face should be found. It is therefore recommended, to cover the top part of the head up to the forehead, and to study and compare only the facial traits. Whether the face falls out somewhat fuller or narrower, plays with regard to the possible changes (see page 25) no essential role. It is however of importance to pay attention, whether a double chin, ears or shoulder plates are similar. Likewise an especially well-formed nose (recognized when viewing from the side) can also be an important reference (see examples page 83).

Also very informative is, if the painting is similar. Here every detail of the eyes, eyebrows - even the dotted corner of the eyes, the mouth, the modelled hair and decorations should be compared. If the painting does not agree or only partially, it is still no counterevidence, for the painting styles were not only general but also within the individual porcelain factories not always similar, they were also altered. If however the painting is similar, it is therefore an evidence that it came from this

An old raw model from the company Hertel, Schwab & Co., shows similarities with the doll below, which therefore was easily identified.

Shoulder head made from bisque, no markings, painted eyes, cloth body, 11-5/8in (30 cm) large, manufactured by the company Hertel, Schwab & Co..

Shoulder head made from china, without markings, manufactured by the company Bähr & Pröschild (see page 174, raw model lower left), small bow in front in the hair, 4-1/2in (11 cm) large

Rear view of the above doll head with the modelled wide braids (color greatly abraded), approx. 1875, two holes for stitching in front and behind.

Shoulder head made from china - modelled blond hair style with 3 curls on the forehead (called in America "Little Girl with three Curls") - painted blue eyes - cloth body with arms and legs made of stone bisque - 21in (53 cm) large - approx. 1870. Another doll head with similar hair style was found with the markings "S. H. 1008".

manufacturer. Identical glass eyes can likewise be an additional reference, however they cannot be used as proof, since identical glass eyes were used by different Porcelain Factories.

Further references can be the details and peculiarities concerning the modeling of hair styles and decorations, for instance similar modelled curls, bows, flowers or leaves, whereby ones attention should be directed especially to the rear of the head.

Likewise similarities can be found in the color, such as the cobalt blue color or the rare grey hair color. One is limited here, because the colors can not always be presented naturally because of printing.

Sometimes a doll can already be identified by using only one striking feature, more often however one will need several similarities, until one can be really sure. But even a hundred percent identification will not always be possible. It is interesting to be able to pinpoint a certain manufacturer, who may come in question.

Shoulder head made from stone bisque, markings in front on the shoulder plate: "4" - modelled and painted hair style in light beige to brown with decorations: light blue gathered frill over the head, at the back of the head a hair net, fastened at the sides with a Rosette and 2 small tassels - painted blue eyes - closed mouth. A similar head was available with the markings: $\mathcal{G}$ - which was used by the porcelain factory Gera - 4in (10 cm) large.

Doll Bodies

The early porcelain doll heads were attached to numerous kinds of doll bodies made from different materials, of which many were produced commercially in the factories, but also a large part were produced however by the buyers themselves at home.

The bodies existed of wood, leather, porcelain and papermaché, predominantly however of cloth and in later years also out of a mixed mass - the so-called composition - and wax cloth. The wax cloth was later used as an exchange for the useless body. The bodies can be made of only one material, for example of cloth or leather, or also of two, such as leather and cloth or wood and porcelain, but also of three or more materials, and from this emerges such a great number of combinations, that it is impossible to discuss all of these. Bodies were not only made in Germany, but also in foreign countries, e.g. in England and France, and above all in America. With some of these combinations will arise other materials, so that one will always find new variations. Here are some very common combinations as well as rare doll bodies:

Cloth bodies (cloth shell): These doll bodies, belong to the type that were produced at the cheapest price, and are therefore the most frequently found type today. They were produced both industrially (whereby often home workers were used) as well as from the buyers themselves at home. That happened initially by hand but later the factories were the first to use sewing machines, followed by the housewives. We find cloth bodies today together with porcelain heads, which were manufactured around 1840, and there exists no doubt, that some are still found in the original condition.

Most cloth bodies are made of cotton (such as Muslin, Nanking, Shirting, calico) or linen and are stuffed with sawdust, hair, cotton wool and wood wool. The cuts extend from a one-piece or two-piece cloth body with cut arms and legs, up to the patchwork body made up of many stitched pieces. The most popular cloth body however was unquestionably those, whose upper arms and upper legs consisted of cloth or leather, and the lower arms and lower legs were made from porcelain (china, later parian or bisque), the latter often found with painted garters and modelled boots or shoes (with or without heels), painted in many different colors, sometimes also with gold luster, in violet and purple. Quite often stockings, leather boots (leg boots) or shoes were sewn on to the leg to save cloth.

Further variations of the bodies included the cloth hull with leather arms and hands, the fingers were either individually sewn on or only back stitched. Arms and legs could be made completely or partially out of wood, papermaché or from composition. Again other doll bodies had a corset, which could be worked in either separately or into the material.

One can recognize the professionally made bodies, because they are made from one type of material, have slender waists and broad hips and are made far more perfectly than the home-made doll bodies. They are distinct with their uneven proportions and are often put together far more wrong than right. That is why we occasionally find today rather strange cloth bodies - too broad or too narrow - with rather short legs or with legs that are far too long. It is rare to find excellent home-made bodies.

Cloth body with lower arms made of brown leather, legs made of reddish material with sewn on leather boots.

Cloth body with lower arms made of bisque and with sewn on black-red cloth legs with laced boots.

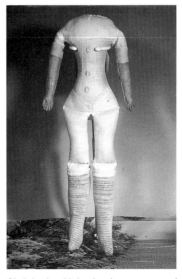

Cloth body with leather lower arms and a worked in corset as well as stockings.

Leather body

Leather body with lower arms made of bisque.

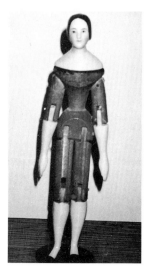

Wood pin or wood splice body with movable china lower arms and legs with painted shoes.

Leather bodies (leather shell). These bodies belonged mainly to the commercially manufactured expensive doll bodies; consist predominantly of white or in rare cases also of pink goatskin, occasionally also made of sheepskin; and have an inside lining made from cloth. They were stuffed with cork or sawdust, hair or wood wool. These leather bodies were at first rather stiff, however they soon had gusset joints, later nailed and rivetted joints, and before 1900 leather ball and socket jointed bodies were produced.

Around 1840, "stiff and movable doll bodies with white leather" were advertised and used for porcelain doll heads. In this case the hull as well as arms and legs were made from leather; the fingers were either back stitched or individually sewn on, the toes as a rule were only implied with several back stitches. The doll heads were attached mainly by glueing them onto the cloth and then sewing the leather around it.

The most beautiful and most popular leather bodies were made - like the cloth bodies - with upper arms made from leather or cloth and the lower arms made from porcelain (china, parian or bisque), while porcelain legs are rarely to be found, evidently rarely used. This is due to the fact that the porcelain legs were constantly banging each other, breaking far more easily than the arms. Therefore one used for the leather bodies far more frequently wooden arms and legs or upper arms and legs made from cloth or leather and lower arms and legs made from wood, papermaché or composition. Many different combinations occurred, as with cloth bodies.

Furthermore cloth-leather bodies also were manufactured with the limbs and the hull made from leather and cloth.

With low-priced leather bodies we can find stockings, boots or shoes with or without heels sewn onto the legs. Usually the cloth below was saved.

Wax-cloth bodies were mostly manufactured in the same way as the leather bodies and at first glance look the same. Often one recognizes them from the structure of the inside of the cloth.

Wooden bodies: Among these today the very rare wooden pegged body was the earliest, which was already used around 1840 for porcelain heads. These bodies were manufactured as a rule industrially. They were made from wooden parts, which were connected using small pegs, so that all limbs were movable. Other wooden bodies, far more primitive and mostly privately produced, consisted of wooden parts, connected with each other and with the porcelain head using wires or pegs.

Motschmann type bodies are extremely rare. This type was copied from a Chinese doll body and represented a baby or child body. This body was registered in 1857 as a patent. The body consisted of either a shoulder plate or swivel plate head, lower arms and legs, as well as the lower body made from porcelain with upper arms and legs. as well as the middle piece of the body made from cloth or leather. A voice box was placed in the middle piece of the body.

All these bodies are original, if they originated from the same period as the doll heads. While one can recognize the original condition of later dolls for swivel heads a Kestner head made of porcelain sits on a right sized Kestner body made from composition. One can not say as a rule that earlier heads belong to a certain type of body. This is due to the fact, that a very large portion of the doll heads were sold individually, which meant that everybody could produce their own doll bodies. As far as one knows all other manufacturers bought doll heads and placed them on their own different bodies. An exception is the Motschmann type body, which being a typical child's body needed a child's head.

Further complications in checking the original condition are the later repairs that were made. Limbs were exchanged frequently, because first the porcelain arms and legs broke and second the leather and cloth hands quickly became dirty and unsavory. To exchange them was no great problem. One could either produce such parts oneself or bring the doll into a doll clinic, which has a large stock of spare parts. One could buy almost all parts there, including all types of arms and legs - for repairing at home or to have them replaced immediately by the expert doll doctor.

One can speak of original condition, if a doll body existed completely of the same or proper old material (e.g. Motschmann type body and wooden body with porcelain arms and legs). The original condition can not be excluded, if the limbs, e.g. from cloth or leather bodies are made from different old materials, as in the combinations indicated. The original condition can be excluded, if it is recognizeable, that the limbs or parts of the body originated from a later period.

However the collector should consider, that many of the early separately sold doll heads never owned a body, and therefore today there is a great lack of old doll bodies. It is appropriate, not to have such large claims and to accept at least old repairs and spare parts. One can not speak of an original condition anymore, but instead of an old condition.

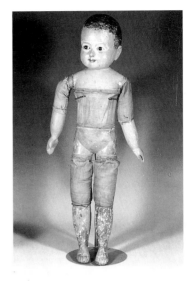

Here a Motschmann type body with wooden parts, also available with china parts.

Leather body in fragile condition, upper body strengthened with material.

Leather body with old bodice and underpants (the so-called inexpressible).

Lower legs made from parian with modelled stockings, blue painted garters, painted pink-black laced boots with heels.

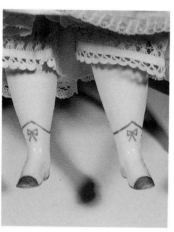

Lower legs made from china with light blue painted boots with heels.

Lower legs made from china with red shoes with gold lustre.

Lower legs made from parian with modelled stockings, painted blue garters and black painted boots.

Lower legs made from china with painted decorative shoes.

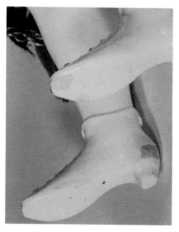

Lower legs made from china with unpainted modelled boots with heels.

High brown leather laced boots.

Brown leather buttoned boots.

Black-red cloth lower legs; sewn on black cloth laced boots.

Brown leather clasp shoe with heel.

Flat clasp shoes with Rosettes.

Flat brown laced shoes.

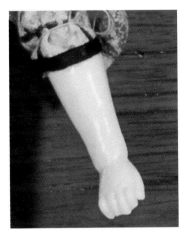

Lower arm made from china, back of hand.

Lower arm made from china, inside of hand.

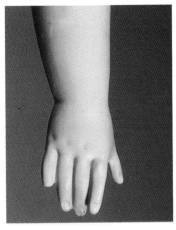

A pair of lower arms made from bisque with very beautifully modelled hands.

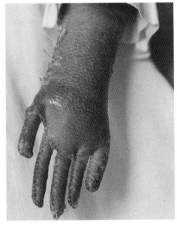

Brown leather hand with individually sewn fingers.

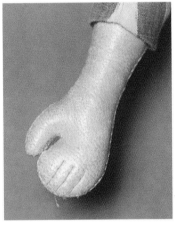

Doll hand made of light colored leather with separate thumb, fingers indicated by stitching.

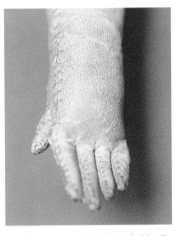

Leather lower arm with individually sewn fingers.

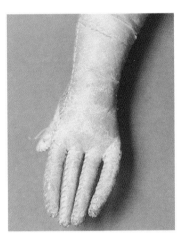

Leather lower arm with individually sewn fingers.

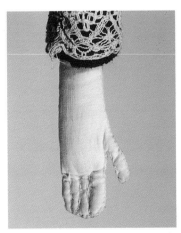

Cloth hand with sewn fingers, only the thumb is individually sewn.

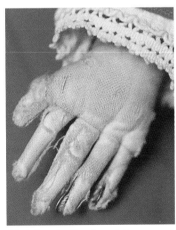

Cloth hand with wire reinforcement, individually sewn fingers.

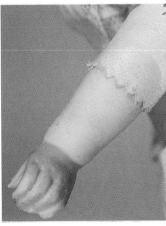

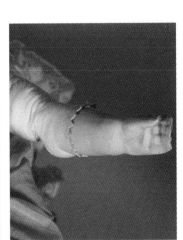

Small bisque lower arms; on the left back of hand, on the right the inside of hand.

Self portrait of the famous French painter Elisabeth Vigée-Lebrun with daughter.

Head made from china modeled after the above-mentioned portrait, markings: 42, which was attributed to the company Dressel, Kister & Co. .

A very expressive shoulder head made from china, a so-called Jenny Lind doll, see also page 48.

Portrait dolls

Even a hundred years after the invention, people are still charmed by the "white fascination" of porcelain, and it is still valued as a precious material, which was used only for fine objects. Slowly however it also became accessible to a wider group of buyers.

As the porcelain manufacturers authorized for the first time their modellers, to create designs for doll heads made from porcelain, it was very clear to them, that dolls with childrens faces promised not to be a great business. This was due largely to economic difficulties. There were not a large number of families who could afford to buy their children such precious and fragile toys. Of course one sees paintings of the 1840s that show children holding a porcelain doll in their arms, but alone that the circumstance, pointed to wealth. Less wealthy citizens could not afford these luxury dolls.

Since the production of childlike doll heads still had subordinate meaning in the first decades after 1840, the manufacturers tried to steer the interests of adults to specially skillful and fine lady heads. Inspirations for their models were found among famous women figures, which stood out in the center of general interest or had already become a legend. There were royalties like Queen Victoria, Queen Luise, Empress Eugénie, Empress Auguste or popular and revered artists like Fanny Elßler and Jenny Lind, later on also literary figures like "Alice in Wonderland" or "Highland Mary".

If one compares today the faces of such portrait dolls with paintings or photographs of their models, it will appear, that the facial traits have probably not been modeled. As a rule one took an already available lady-like or childlike model head, altered it somewhat and tried above all to produce recognizeable features, such as hair styles or special jewelry or head gear, that were well known attributes to the personality. This meant, that the faces were not modelled exactly after human models. It also speaks for the fact, that many of these heads with identical faces were manufactured with different hair styles, head gears or decorations.

The names, under which these so-called portrait dolls are known today, were received only very recently from collectors, who were looking for a name, so that they could communicate among themselves. However most of the names originated from the original period of the doll making.

In reference to Fanny Essler it is reported, that during a show in 1844 a so-called Fanny Essler doll was presented, which had been created especially for this show. Unfortunately it is not known, whether Fanny Essler had stood perhaps as a model for this. The hair style is however authentic.

Also in reference to Jenny Lind there is a document of that period, which says, that in 1850 the first expected Jenny Lind dolls had finally arrived by ship to America.

Both ladies were celebrated artists, who displaced their period in a true rapture of enthusiasm. Fanny Essler was a dancer and Jenny Lind a singer. Their expertise was connected with beauty, charm and esprit, but modesty and charity also were the causes for their unusual popularity. The idea was that this spirit should be captured and immortalized in the creation of a doll. The public's response provided a good market for such a collectible.

Some of these dolls with this name are presented on pages 42,43,48 and 49 along with photos of their models. One can decide if there really is a similarity!

One of the first portrait and porcelain head dolls was the so-called "Queen Victoria" doll. However her features are not identical with the model. The hair style, the Queen wore was wavy at the sides and then pulled back to be braided and then fashioned at the rear of the head into a wreath. The doll has brown or black, modelled and painted hair, the skin color has a slight hint of soft pink luster, and the neck is rather long. There is also a young Victoria with braids (see middle illustration).

Shoulder head made from pink toned china after Queen Victoria.

One of the earliest, most well-known and by far the most frequently found parian doll is called "Dagmar" or "Countess Dagmar" and represents the Danish Princess Dagmar, who married in 1866 the subsequent Russian Czar Alexander III and was mother of the late Czar Nikolaus II.

To the earliest childlike dolls belong "Alice in Wonderland", who had emerged as the main figure out of the fairy-tale from the English poet Lewis Carroll. According to the model of Sir John Tenniel illustrated first edition of the book, the hair was combed to the rear and was held by a hair band.

The "Highland Mary" is a more childlike, more girlish doll head with short page style hair. The model for this was the dead girlfriend made immortal in the poem of the late Scottish poet Robert Burns. Already in 1792 she became rather popular in a song about a lovely girl from the Scottish highland:

China shoulder head after Queen Victoria with braids over the head - called "young Victoria".

> ... The golden hours on angel wings,
> they flew past for you and me - my darling,
> as dearly for me as light and lives -
> was my sweet Highland Mary. ..

Through this song she attained so much popularity, that this doll was named after her.

Around the same period as the "Highland Mary", there emerged other doll heads, which we know today under the name "Empress Eugénie", "Queen Luise" and "Empress Augusta". Similarities with the faces of the models are hardly found, however there are certain references on particular features. The Empress Eugénie dolls wear, from which there are several versions, the same hair styles, of the Empress (see page 52, 53), or certain types of head gear associated with royal positions. Empress Eugénie was one of the exciting phenomena of the 19th Century.

Queen Luise again is known through the blue veil (blue scarf) (see page 56, 57). As one can see on paintings, she always carried a veil draped artistically around the head, and it is said, that she tried to conceal a small disfigurement at the throat. Queen Luise, who had a very short life - she died at the age of 34 - was grieved and idolized by her people as she was the only Prussian Queen. Empress Augusta can easily be recognized by her characteristic hair style with diadem and the cross at the throat. She was the first woman in Germany, who was presented with the iron cross from the Emperor.

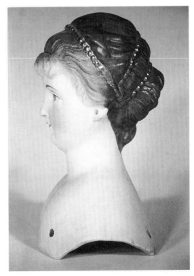

Profile of a bisque head, which was named after the 3 modelled beads the Parthenia type, which entwine the hair style.

Nanking dolls

Nanking doll - shoulder head, lower arms and legs are made of china, the body made from Nanking material.

Around 1860 Nanking dolls appeared on the market. Although the name suggests a Chinese origin one deals by no means with Chinese dolls. The name refers rather to the material of the bodies, which was produced mostly from a cheap red-brownish cotton wool, the so-called Nanking. The head, lower arms and legs were made of simple quality glazed porcelain, later also out of parian and bisque. The bodies were sewn commercially (widely in home work) and filled mostly with sawdust. The porcelain factories either sold complete dolls or only porcelain parts.

As can be seen from old catalogs and advertisements today, they were more of a low-priced mass product and were mostly unpretentious dolls, produced by almost all porcelain factories for export. From an advertisement from the eighties of the 19th Century can be seen, that they were sold not only with glazed porcelain heads and simple, black painted hair styles but also in parian and bisque with different hair styles and hair colors, glass eyes and painted boots. The dolls was either dressed or undressed and available in several sizes. They were delivered rather cheaply in simple quality at the dozen.

In front of the photograph of a child from around 1900 two dressed Nanking dolls sitting side by side from the same period.

Doll Clothes

The charm and attractiveness of a doll did not only depend on the beauty and expressiveness of their head, but was closely connected with the overall appearance - especially with what she wore. Most collectors have recognized this distinction already and pay high prices for a beautiful originally equipped doll with extravagant old clothes.

This is not extraordinary or by any means rare, that one paid far more for the clothes than for the doll itself. Indeed this case was only for French dolls, and it rarely happened for German dolls. Therefore it is not astounding, that many collectors show themselves discontented today with the accessories of their early porcelain and parian dolls, which are badly dressed and look less attractive. Of course it should be the uppermost law, to keep and protect these old clothes, nevertheless one should take into consideration, that collectors would like to rejoice at the sight of their dolls. So it is quite understandable, if they remove these unattractive clothes - and hopefully preserve them carefully - and go out and buy a more attractive wardrobe or trousseau for their old doll.

Outsiders will object, that there is no real art, in sewing a new doll dress, as collectors and sewing advocates explain that there is no greater experience then to reproduce fashionable doll clothes from the era. The work is successful, if after one looks at it repeatedly he can not decide if the clothes are genuinely old or only reproduced. One does not have to be a seamstress, but one must have some creative flair and the right eye for old materials.

Since there are some collectors, who are not quite clear, what is meant by original clothes and the differences in the old clothes, original clothes can be defined as the clothes, with which the doll was sold in a shop, or, if it was sold unclothed, then old clothes of that period.

There are main points that the collector should consider about the charm of old doll clothes. Independent of the fact that the clothes of that period were far more complicated in design and much more extravagant, the magic is that the colors have faded and the materials have become thin, delicate and threadbare. There lies a layer of dust over their 100 years existence, and so a wave of romanticism and nostalgia passes over us, and that is what we as collectors and preservers of old things, want to keep and pass on to other generations.

To get a certain feeling for old doll clothes, one should look at the originals again and again, so as to study them, and memorize their style, namely that the colors are far more modest, the materials and lace far more finer, the patterns and folds smaller - that everything is true to scale for dolls.

The only question is: where can one still find original clothes? The happy collectors, who still own beautiful original wardrobes and extravagant old doll clothes for their early dolls, are very rare. In the course of over a hundred years a lot of clothes have fallen apart and have been thrown away. In addition many doll ladies have never owned an original commercial wardrobe, because one bought only the porcelain heads and limbs and produced the bodies as well as the clothes personally at home. Also at doll fairs ar.. markets dolls in old or original clothes

Three illustrations of a doll from approx. 1880, which is still in its original condition. The dress is made of gossamer like, gauzy cotton material, ...

... the under garments made from somewhat thicker material ...

... the doll is sewn into it completely. It is 10in (25cm) large (see also page 52, centre row on the left).

A doll boy with bisque shoulder head in old Scotish clothes.

An example for the doll fashion of the previous century three reworked dresses for small

dolls. In this one case new material was used, since old materi-

als would tear immediately when dressing.

have become very rare. The simplest method still is, to thumb through doll books, in which original wardrobes are illustrated, and to look at old prints, paintings, or patterns in museums. With time the look will sharpen itself more and more for the differences between newly made and old clothes.

To produce new clothes for the doll ladies and bring out their full beauty is what we speak of mostly here. Requirements for this are beautiful old doll like materials, and naturally time and patience for searching at doll fairs, at flee-markets, at antique shows and elsewhere. The search can be very entertaining and in addition create nice contacts to similar-minded collectors.

Here are a couple of tips: Should a suitable fitting doll dress be made, one should only concentrate on the doll head. A lady head with extravagant hair style (flowers, feathers, jewelry etc.) is suitable for a splendid party dress or a ball gown made from velvet, silk or brocade, one should pay attention to whether the style for the beautiful shoulder plate is free or covered to decide on a style for the gown. It is also recommended, to bring out the beauty of the porcelain arms, while one covers unsightly leather or cloth arms with sleeves, tip cuffs or gloves. With modelled upper parts color and style should absolutely match and the pattern cut should fit the modelling. For lady heads with hats or bonnets one should look for a pretty costume made from light weight wool, cotton-wool or velvet in the style of that period, and dolls with childrens heads should have a childlike dress, where the lace panties can be seen. For dolls with boy-like or men's heads a trim contemporary suit should be produced out of velvet, silk or cloth.

Since the old materials used are mostly fragile, one should line them with a thin, but firm material. This is not difficult to do if one places both materials on top of each other, holds it down with pins, cuts and sews together. Also the underwear should not be forgotten, since the petticoats are a very important piece for the beautiful old clothes.

If one has bought with love and a good eye everything that is needed, one should not worry about the expense, so that a beautiful old doll again receives its appropriate attire. The success at the sight of the new dressed doll will not vanish! Perhaps all the trouble has been profitable for the future, and the carefully attired doll stands one day with these clothes in a museum. Lastly the pursuit of doll clothes is so versatile, that it even can become its own collecting area.

Values

The reference point of value given within this book are intended as value guides rather than fixed prices because doll prices are constantly changing. The assigning of collector's relative values of low, medium and high indicate desirability.

Since some collectors collect only doll heads of the kind shown in this book and set them up like busts, or others collect only whole dolls, a separate method of appraisal is given here.

Doll heads: The values for doll heads with modelled hair vary from style to style, the quality of materials that the doll is made from and desirability.

Lower value class: In this value class belong doll heads made from minor quality porcelain such as cruder, spotted porcelain (with iron oxide or other spots), with very simply modelled hair styles and various decorations (such as implied bows, bands or flowers), with simple painting, and painted eyes as well as the smaller simpler heads.

Medium value class: In this value class belong doll heads made from good porcelain with extravagant modelled hair styles and various decorations as well as good painting (e.g. red eyelid strokes), with painted eyes or with glass eyes.

Upper value class: In this value class belong doll heads made only from the finest porcelain, whose artistic appearance lifts them out clearly from the remaining doll heads, such as the heads made by KPM. Furthermore such heads exemplify extravagant modelled hair styles and various decorations (e.g. with jewelry in the hair, particular head gears, modelled upper parts), possibly with decorations (such as frills, flowers, leaves), with glass eyes but also with painted eyes. Many of the early glazed doll heads are valued higher and can achieve collectors prices due to their rareness, age, pink tone, and if they display marks of the Royal Porcelain Manufactures.

Further criteria for a high value are: *particular beauty, expressiveness, good contours, unusualness* and *rarity*. The size of these doll heads also play a role in the value. Larger doll heads are more expensive than small ones. This lies in the fact, that they were manufactured in smaller quantities and are usually of higher quality. Besides all the fine details and modelling can be seen far more better with a large head, and on the other hand richer decorations could be well formed - especially if they were made by hand - easily applied, glazed far better and are painted far more effectively.

Glass eyes: Early doll heads with glass eyes are rated rarer than such with painted eyes and have therefore a higher value. This is quite true, although one should not value it too highly, for many collector's agree, that heads, which have painted hair and painted eyes, have a more harmonious impression than such with glass eyes.

Furthermore the *condition* plays a large role. Damages like cracks, hairline

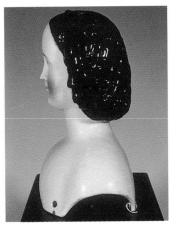

For this doll head from approx. 1870, with the stately size of 8in (20cm), an appropriate price (according to quality) would be set in the medium price range. A smaller head would cost however far less.

Doll bodies (without head) made from leather with lower arms made from bisque: price according to size.

fractures, blisters or chipped faces and bodies can according to size and availability reduce the value, this also counts for firing mistakes. Restorations also hurt the value, especially if they have been done badly. To restore in such a case the beauty of an old head, one would have to remove the bad restoration, which could lead to new damages. Still it is profitable to take into account when buying a very early and rare doll the restorations and damages, if they have not destroyed the beauty of the face. Ultimately one can not wait here like with other later doll heads for better preserved pieces, because one would have to wait a very long time. Indeed the damages should be clearly taken out of the value.

Doll bodies: A doll body is rated according to its age, its condition, its style and its material. The latter means, that for example a simple cloth body with sewn arms and legs is valued at the lowest, while a leather body from the same period lies with its value higher. That does not exclude, that an excellent cloth body can be more expensive than a bad leather body, an individual appraisal is alone decisive. The material that the limbs are made from and finishing techniques also affect values. Porcelain arms can be valued more and porcelain legs, possibly with painted gold luster boots can cost the same. Wood pegged bodies, as well as Motschmann type bodies are especially rare and hard to find. Extraordinary bodies can be found in a higher value bracket.

Whole dolls: They achieve according to attire a higher value because a whole all original doll is rated far more valuable than individual parts. Dolls at the lower value class are calculated at present with two thirds of the buying price for the doll head and a third for the body plus accessories. This formula can not be used however in the high price class, because it can happen, that an expensive head is attached to a cheap body. Here a total appraisal must result for originality and quality, which results in higher value, since whole remaining dolls are very rare to find. In such a case the entire doll is used for determining the value. Naturally the accessories - of clothes, underwear, shoes, stockings accessories etc. also play a significant role, and so an all original doll attains a far higher value.

Doll with china head and lower arms from approx. 1870 in old dress. Price for such dolls determined according to size, quality and outfit.

Explanations to the Illustration Section

All information about the dolls in this book resulted of our own extensive knowledge and research on the subject. In some cases they could not be completed, since some of these dolls have been bought by unknown persons. Some museums and collectors rightfully refused, to take off their dolls clothes for more exact research or to take off the heads, because a certain risk in damaging the head, bodies or clothes was connected.

Markings, which are found as a rule on or in the shoulder plates, are indicated, as far as they were available and known to us.

Since most of the photographs are of large format one can recognize the details very clearly, thus saving some troublesome descriptions. Exceptions and particularities are pointed out however.

Facts, that are correct as a rule for all dolls, are not repeated every time, such as:
all doll heads have modelled and painted hair;
the **mouth** of the doll heads are - outside of a few exceptions - modelled **closed** and painted;
the doll heads have **painted eyes**, if not indicated explicitly as glass eyes, as a rule fine painting, can be observed at best from the illustrative material;
the **doll bodies** and **clothes** are either old or produced from old material.

The doll names were adopted mainly from the American collectors. Only the most common and well known ones were selected.

In this book we presented predominantly rare and exclusive dolls, which would exemplify a very beautiful, wonderful, delightful rare doll. However with all these dolls these expressions would have to be constantly repeated; therefore we have left them out.

As in other collector's literature, we have quite often used the expression "attributed" in this book, only then, there are featured doll heads, that point to a certain manufacturer. The doll head remains attributed to this company as long as or until the contrary is proven.

My investigations, which refer to raw models, only include dolls found on factory grounds through excavation or the tearing down of buildings. The old raw models were cleaned carefully to remove all dirt, since the details would not have been otherwise recognizeable. The new raw models were made from old, greatly worn out molds, where the modelling of the rear of the head was quite often destroyed. Raw models and molds, found on general refuse dumps, whose origin was not exactly known, have not been considered.

A so-called Mary Todd doll, see page 44 for further description.

Fanny Elssler

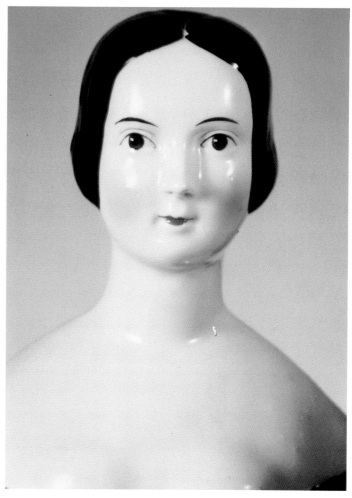

Front view ...   ... and profile of the Fanny Elssler doll.

Portrait of the dancer Fanny Elssler.

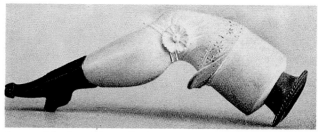

A copy of the leg of Fanny Elssler as an ivory cigarette holder.

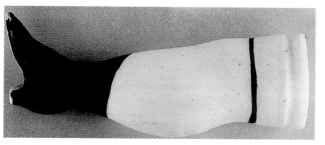

Such doll legs were produced in different types of china, possibly inspired by the leg of Fanny Elssler.

Fanny Elssler

Shoulder head made of glazed, flesh tinted china. Hair is double parted on top, coming together at the hairline to form a "V" shape. Smooth black hair swoops down to cover the ears and is caught up in a coiled, braided bun in back. Brown painted eyes with indicated corners, eyelid strokes and nose dots in red. Closed mouth painted red. Long neck, well modeled breasts, deep shoulder plate with three sewing holes in front and back. Cloth body with china lower arms and legs. This fine china doll has no visible marks. 22in (56 cm), circa 1850.

These so-called Fanny Elssler dolls show several important criteria, which attributes them to the above-mentioned company, and these are seen both in the painting as well as the similarity in the modelling of the face of the "Mary Todd" (see page 44, above right). With the above-mentioned head it is clearly recognizable, that it was copied from KPM.

Mary Todd

Shoulder head made from parian - blond painted hair style and modelled blue bows at the side, modelled black hair band and hair net at the back of the head - painted blue eyes - automatic body made from papermaché with metal hands - 10in (25 cm) large - approx. 1870 - a so-called Mary Todd in Parian.

Early version of the so-called Mary Todd - shoulder head made from china, flesh tinted china - black painted hair style with modelled black bows (one on each side), modelled hair band over the head and very fine hair net at the back of the head - long neck - model led breasts - painted blue eyes, with circular line painted corners of the eye and modelled eyelids - closed modelled mouth, whose painting displays a white gap - the head is 8in (20 cm) large - not glazed on the inside - approx. 1860.

Front and back view of the raw model show the similarities of the modelling with both side bows, the modelled hair band over the head and the hair net at the back of the head. With the head in the illustration above on the right the bows, hair band and hair net have not been painted and the latter falls out a bit smaller.

Back of the head of the Mary Todd doll described on page 45.

Mary Todd

Shoulder head made from glazed china, white china - painted black hair with two partially gilded hair bows as well as modelled band over the head and hair net with gold lustre at the back of the head - painted blue eyes, with circular line painted corners of the eye - two holes for sewing in front and back - body completely made from cloth - 12-3/4in (45 cm) large - approx. 1865.
This doll type, which is called in America "Mary Todd Lincoln" or in short "Mary Todd" was named after the wife of Abraham Lincoln. It is found in several different versions and types of china, of which we have presented on both pages here three different types.

Shoulder head made from china, flesh tinted china with orange tinted cheeks and pink dabs at the throat and shoulders - marked on the inside with a "4" - black painted hair style - painted blue eyes, eyelids slightly modeled - size of head 4-1/2in (11.5 cm) - approx. 1860.

The reflection shows the back of the head of the "Grape Lady" (page 47) with the modelled hair net.

Rear view of the doll head (from above on the left), which is identical with the raw model (on the right).

Front view of the same raw model.

Grape Lady

Exquisite shoulder head made from glazed china, skin color white china - black painted hair style with white frill, edged with lavender color and gold lustre, at the back of the head a hair net with gold lustre - painted blue eyes with modelled eyelids, half circle shaped painted corners of the eye and red eyelid strokes - the painting of the closed modelled mouth shows a narrow white gap - three sewing holes at the front and back - cloth body with porcelain lower arms and legs - 21in (53.3cm) large - approx. 1865.

This type was produced in different versions, most frequently it is decorated with blue grapes, and therefore it is called by collectors the "Grape Lady". Here the rare version with pink-red fruit; there is also however one with flower decorations. Because of the similarity of the face with other doll heads from the above-mentioned company as well as the similarities in the painting, this doll was attributed to the company Alt, Beck & Gottschalck.

Jenny Lind

A portrait of the singer Jenny Lind, who was called also the "Swedish Nightingale".

The reflection of the so-called Jenny Lind doll shows the details of the back of the head.

Expressive head made from china, another so-called Jenny Lind doll - cloth body - 19-3/4in (50 cm) large - approx.1870.

Back of the head of the above-mentioned doll, the broken raw model next to it both show similar modelling.

Jenny Lind

Shoulder head made from glazed china, black painted hair style with middle parting, hair in wavy long hair strands, which stand out at the sides rather widely, combed to the rear and shaped into a wreath - painted blue eyes with modelled eyelids and red eyelid strokes - cloth body with leather arms - 21in (53 cm) large - approx. 1860.
Dolls with this typical type of hair style are called "Jenny Lind". A very interesting and popular doll, which is also found with similar blond hair style.

Miss Liberty

A beautiful profile of the doll on the opposite page.

Old broken raw model (Front - and rear view), which is identical with the doll head (on the right), and from which the doll "Miss Liberty" could be identified.

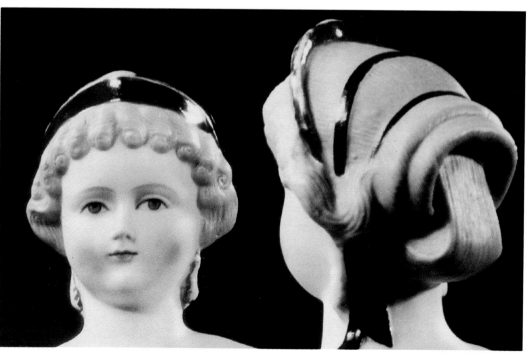

The reflection, shows the hair style, which is modelled rather lavishly at the back of the head and is entwined with a black hair band.

Miss Liberty

Shoulder head made from very pale bisque - hair style adorned with a gold lustre diadem - painted blue eyes with eyelashes (latter rarely found with painted eyes) however without eyelid strokes - modelled on earrings in white with gold lustre (likewise very rare) - 16 1/2in (42 cm) large - approx. 1875 - cloth body with bisque forearms and lower legs.
This doll because of the similarities with the head of the Statue of Liberty in New York is called "Miss Liberty".

Empress Eugénie

Portrait of the Empress Eugénie.

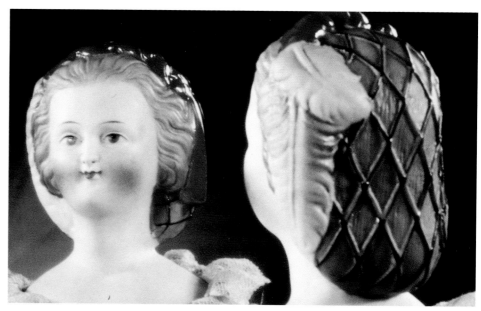

Shoulder head made from Parian - variation of the empress Eugénie type - hair style identical to that of the doll pictured on the opposite page, hair net with knots - old cloth body - 17 1/2in (44.5 cm) large - approx. 1870.

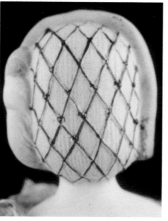

Shoulder head made from Parian - a simple version of the empress Eugénie doll - 10in (25 cm) large - hair net with knots.

Full view of the doll pictured on the opposite page.

The back of the head with the hair net without knots.

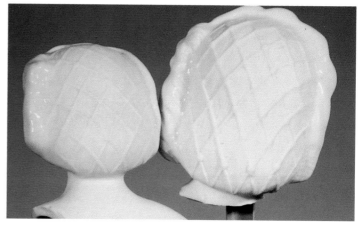

Front and rear view of raw models, which are identical with the Empress Eugénie dolls. The details of the modelling are very visible , e.g. the rear of the head with the hair net, one with and one without knots in the hair net.

Empress Eugénie

Shoulder head made from Parian - the blond painted hair style is decorated with a modelled draped shawl and a feather at the side with lustre, at the back of the head a hair net without knots, very fine painting in very delicate colors - painted eyes with eyelashes, however without eyelid strokes - two sewing holes in front and behind - leather bodies with bisque forearms - 17 3/4in (45 cm) large - approx. 1870 - a so-called Empress Eugénie doll. The beautiful and elegant french Empress Eugénie was the wife of Napoleon III, this doll was named after her.

Empress Augusta

Profile,

Back of the head ...

... and full view of the Empress Augusta doll.

Empress Augusta

Shoulder head made from bisque with painted blond hair style and modelled on pearl jewelry, modelled blouse upper part with pink stripes (also found with blue stripes) and black cross - painted blue eyes - two sewing holes in front and behind - leather body with bisque forearms - 23 3/4in (60 cm) large - around 1880 - a so-called Empress Augusta doll, also known with brown or black hair - besides there is also a similar head without the modelled blouse upper part - due to similarities in the face, modelling and painting, this doll is attributed to the above named company.

Queen Luise (Blue Scarf) Marking: 894 # 6

Pictures above and below: Two paintings of Queen Luise, which show her with a veil around the neck.

Shoulder head made from Parian, markings: 894 # 6, with modelled blue shawl after Queen Luise of Prussia - known in America under the name "blue scarf" - painted blue eyes - cloth body - 19in (48 cm) large - around 1870.

Back of the head with the beautifully modelled long curls of the Queen Luise doll.

Queen Luise (Blue Scarf)   Marking: 894

Shoulder head made from Parian with painted blond curled hair style and modelled blue veil (blue scarf) after Queen Luise of Prussia - markings: 894 - blue glass eyes with paperweight effect - cloth body with bisque lower arms and legs - 17 1/2in (44.5 cm) large - around 1870.

Two shoulder heads made from Parian with identical modelled hair style and modelled flat pillbox with feather - both are identical, except for the hair style, to the raw models shown below from the above-mentioned company - both 17 3/4in (45 cm) large - approx. 1880.

Shoulder head made from Parian with modelled hat with rose and feather - at the back of the head a series of modelled curls, which can be seen on the raw models below - cloth body - 8 3/4in (22 cm)

Front and rear view of a raw model, whose pillbox is identical to both dolls, pictured above, however the hair style of the above-mentioned dolls are identical with the raw model pictured on the right.

Front and rear view of a raw model, which is identical with the doll pictured on the right above.

Two almost identical raw models, of which the right one is identical to the doll pictured on page 59.

Back of the head of the raw model, which is identical with the back of the head of the doll pictured on page 59.

Full view of the doll pictured on the right - she is wearing an old silk dress and modelled, painted black shoes without heels.

Shoulder head made from Parian with modelled feather hat - this doll head is a variation of the type Empress Eugénie - painted blue eyes - closed mouth - cloth body with forearms and lower legs made from parian - 9 1/2in (24 cm) large - approx. 1875.

The comparison with the raw models (pictured on the lefthand page) shows, that there is no doubt: These doll heads were produced by the above named company.

Shoulder head made from very pale bisque with modelled black hair band and modelled earrings and necklace; the fine painting is identical with the other heads (pictured on both pages).

Identical shoulder head made from pale bisque, as pictured on the right-hand page, but with painted black hair style - 18in (46 cm) large - approx. 1870.

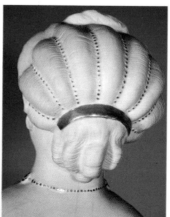

Shoulder head made from Parian with modelled hair band and rose, as well as modelled earrings - painted eyes with painted eyelashes,

Old raw model with molded on rose and modelled earrings, which is identical with the doll pictured on the left.

Back and profile of the head of the doll pictured on page 61 with the lavish hair style, modelled gold colored pearls and comb.

Shoulder head made from very pale bisque - lavish modelled, white hair style with a white and at the edges gilded feather, painted blue eyes with painted eyelashes, but without eyelid strokes - very fine painting, modelled earrings in white and gold - modelled gold colored chain - cloth body with leather arms, individually stepped fingers - 21 3/4in (55 cm) large - approx. 1870.

If one compares the finished produced doll heads on both pages with each other and with the old raw model (bottom row, 2nd from the left), it becomes evident, that all of these heads originated from one company, i.e. Alt, Beck & Gottschalck. It is not only the identical faces but also the identical style of painting, likewise the rare, modelled earrings.

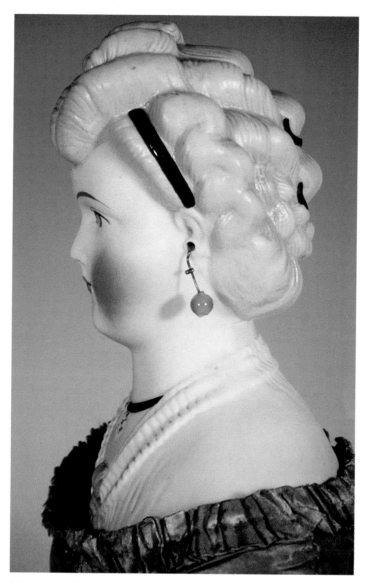

Full view of the doll pictured on the right page with modelled and painted boots.

The pretty profile of the same doll with lavish modelled hair style.

Broken shoulder head, found on the factory land of the above-mentioned company.

Back of the head of the above-mentioned doll.

Shoulder head made from very pale bisque with lavish blond hair style, trimmed with a painted black hair band - modelled upper blouse with blue bow as well as necklace with pendant - painted blue eyes - three sewing holes in front and back - cloth body with leather arms and bisque lower legs - 17 3/4in (45 cm) large - approx. 1880.

The similarities with the broken doll head on the left page (bottom row left, see other changes on page 25) points to the above mentioned company.

Head with detacheable ornamental Diadem

Shoulder head made from Parian with finely modelled blond hair style - extraordinary and rare is the detachable ornamental diadem made from metal, which can be placed into two holes; these holes are also found in the raw model pictured below, which looks slightly different due to the large eye cavities and somewhat modified hair style - the shape of the ears is identical with all three heads (on both pages) - approx. 1875.

Back of the head of the above pictured doll

Front view of the raw model, clearly visible the two holes for attaching the ornamental diadem.

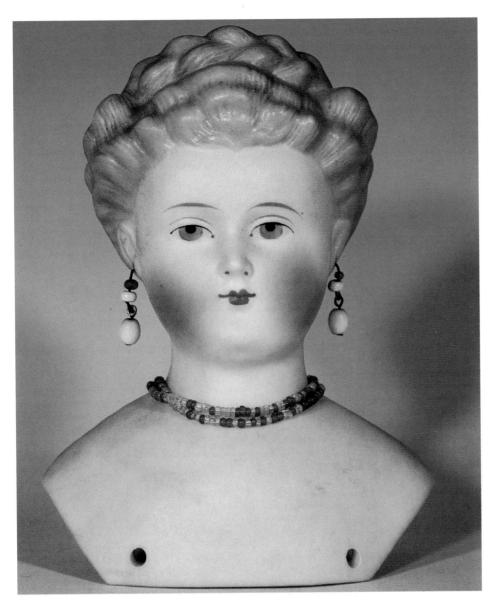

Shoulder head made from bisque - hair style and ears are identical with the raw model pictured below right , but also the similarities with the face of the doll on the opposite page is immense - size of the head 5in (13 cm) - approx. 1885.

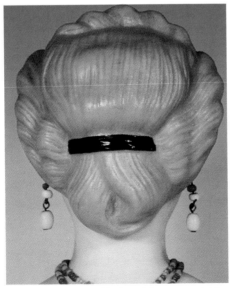

The back of the head (on the right) of the above pictured doll is identical with that of the raw model (on the left). Therefore both doll heads have been identified through the raw model.

Alice in Wonderland

Shoulder head made from bisque with blond painted hair style, modelled hair band and hair net. A variation of the model head of "Alice in Wonderland".

Full view of "Alice in Wonderland" pictured on opposite page, the clothes are possibly original.

Shoulder head made from Parian - a so-called "Alice in Wonderland" - painted blue eyes - leather body - 22in (56 cm) large - approx. 1870.

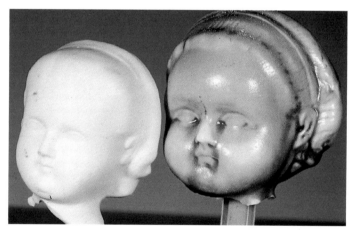

Raw model of a modified "Alice in Wonderland" with hair net.

Two raw models of "Alice in Wonderland", viewed from the front, which are respectively identical with those pictured on page 67 and above on the right.

Back of the head of the above pictured "Alice in Wonderland".

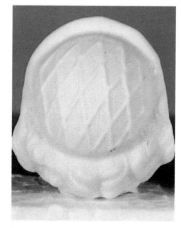

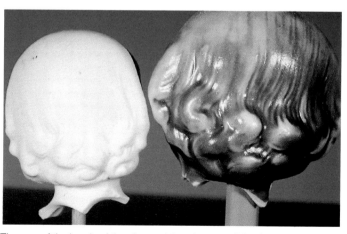

Back of the head of a modified raw model "Alice in Wonderland" with hair net.

The rear of the heads of the above pictured raw models of "Alice in Wonderland".

Alice in Wonderland

Shoulder head made from Parian, typical hair style with modelled black hair band, hair combed back from the forehead - painted eyes - cloth body with leather forearms, fingers individual stepped - 14in (36 cm) large - approx. 1875. Model for this very popular doll was the fairy tale book "Alice in Wonderland", it was produced by several companies. Some of these companies who also produced Alice dolls were for example Simon & Halbig (see page 181, upper row on the right), as well as Hertel, Schwab & Co. (see page 175, upper row).

Marking: 974

Marking: 990 # 10

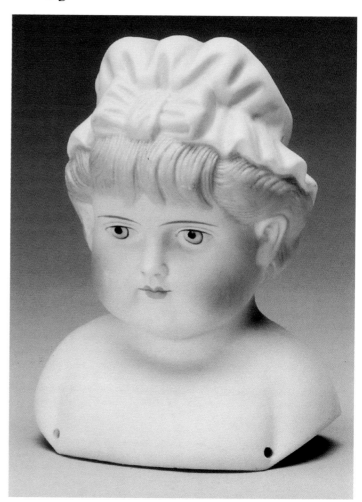

Shoulder head made from Parian with comical standing out ears - markings: 974 - blue glass eyes with paperweight effect - kid leather body - 14in (36 cm) large - approx. 1880.

Shoulder head made from Parian - markings: 990 # 10 - modelled bonnet with bow, identical model to the one pictured on page 69, but only with painted eyes - 5 1/2in (14,5 cm) large - approx. 1880.

Marking: 990

Shoulder head made from Parian with molded bonnet with red bow - markings: 990 - glass eyes with paperweight effect - cloth body with leather arms - 15 3/4in (40 cm) large - 1885.

Marking: 998 # 6

Shoulder head made from bisque with modelled hat - markings: 998 # 6 - size of head 4 3/4in (12 cm) - approx. 1885.

Marking: 996 # 8

Shoulder head made from bisque with modelled violet bonnet and white veil - markings: 996 # 8 - painted eyes - kid leather body - 17 3/4in (45 cm) large - around 1885.

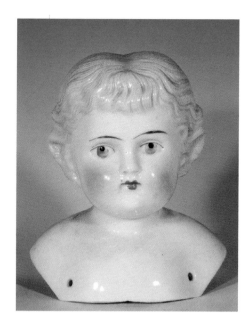

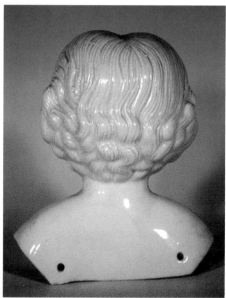

Shoulder head a so-called Highland Mary made from china - painted eyes -size 4 3/4in (12 cm) -

Two "Highland Marys" with bisque shoulder heads and forearms and painted eyes. Original clothing.

A broken head of a Highland Mary as a simple model, found on the above-mentioned companies land.

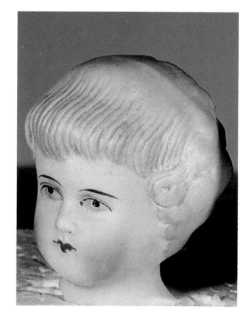

Highland Mary   Marking: 1000 # 10

Shoulder head made from bisque with typical V-shaped folds at the shoulders - a so-called Highland Mary - markings: 1000 # 10 - relatively simple blond hair style (also available with black painted hair) - blue glass eyes with paperweight effect - minute dimple on the chin - cloth body with sewn on leather boots and bisque forearms - 23 3/4in (60 cm) large - approx. 1880 - these dolls found great popularity and are therefore to be found rather frequently today.

Marking: 1054

Full view of the doll pictured on the right.

Shoulder head made from bisque - markings: 1054 - modelled blond curled hair style with modelled blue bonnet - blue glass eyes with painted eyelashes - cloth body - size of head 5 1/2in (14 cm) - around 1880.

Marking: 1024 # 10

Shoulder head made from bisque - markings: 1024 # 10 - simple brown painted hair, modelled orange-red cap with black band and bow - blue glass eyes - cloth body with leather arms - size of head 5 1/2in (14 cm) - around 1880.
This doll, as well as the Queen Luise doll, the Highland Mary and the heads found on the pages 68, 69, 70, 71 and 74 come from the same model head, only the hair styles and head gear have been modelled differently.

Marking: 508

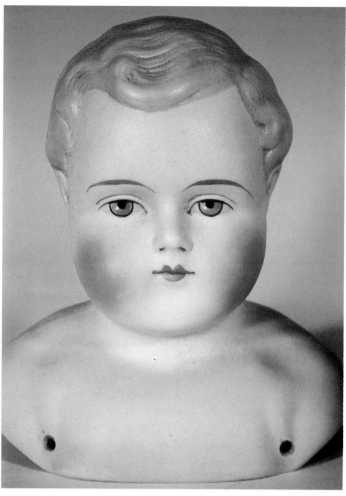

Boy shoulder head made from bisque without markings, (later identical heads have been marked with the number 508) - clearly visible both identically modelled V-shaped folds at the shoulders, which are found rather frequently on shoulder heads produced by Alt, Beck & Gottschalck - 6 1/2in (16 cm) large - approx. 1880.

Simple shoulder head made from Parian - painted eyes - cloth body - 19in (48 cm) large - approx. 1880.

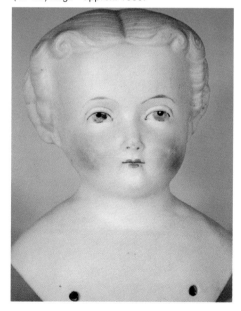

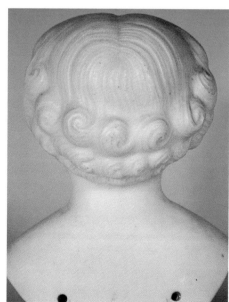

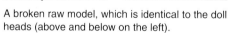

A broken raw model, which is identical to the doll heads (above and below on the left).

Simple shoulder head made from Parian, - painted blue eyes - approx. 1880.

... here the the back of the head

Shoulder head made from bisque with blond painted hair style and with modelled lace cloth as well as modelled neck ruffle with pendant - painted blue eyes - cloth body with forearms made from bisque - 23 3/4in (60 cm) large - approx. 1880.
Because of the similarity of the face, the modelling and painting it is attributed to the above-mentioned company.

Marking:

Shoulder head made from china, white tinted skin color - markings: - painted blue eyes - leather body - 25 1/2in (65 cm) large - approx. 1870.

The back of the head with the beautifully modelled hair style and also the full view of the doll.

The inside of the head with the markings.

Shoulder head made from china without markings - especially skillfully modelled hair style - painted eyes, closed mouth - cloth body - 17 3/4in (45 cm) large - approx. 1870.

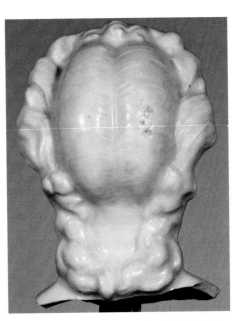

A broken shoulder head made from china, on the right the back of the head - blond painted hair style - painted eyes - closed mouth - size of head 2 1/4in (5.5 cm) - approx. 1870.
Both heads were found on the land of the company Conta & Boehme.

A broken shoulder head made from china with black painted hair style - identical face to the head on the left - the hair style is however identical with the above pictured doll - size 2 1/2 in (6.5 cm) - approx. 1870.

A full view of the doll pictured on the opposite page. She is wearing an original reworked dress made from old material, of light blue silk and cream colored tull, with dark red velvet edges and covered with minute glass pearls, old underwear, shoes and stockings.

An identical doll head, as shown on both of these pages, was found according to the Coleman Encyclopedia Vol. I with this marking from the above-mentioned company. In addition further wonderful doll heads richly decorated with flowers and leaves, partially designed by hand, freely shaped and modelled were found. Because of the similarity of the faces (example see page 83) and the identical modelling and painting I have attributed the following doll heads to the company Dornheim, Koch & Fischer.

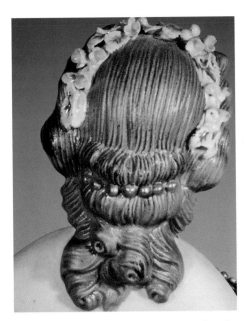

The back of the head with the skillful hair style, adorned with blossom wreath and gold colored pearls.

Shoulder head made from parian in very fine workmanship (Meissen-Genre) - roses, leaves and bell flowers were modelled by hand freely and molded on, while the modelling of the chain was already contained in the mould - the chain is gold colored, the veins of the leaves with pink gold lustre and the hair style is painted brown - eyes painted - 3 sewing holes in front and behind - long narrow cloth body - 19 3/4in (50 cm) large - around 1870.

A beautiful profile of the doll described on pages 80 and 81, clearly visible the modelling of the blossom wreath.

These photos, which present all 7 doll heads in profile, should demonstrate the identical modelling of the faces, above all the thin , little bent noses. Besides that also the similarities are shown in the painting of the faces, the hair, the flowers and leaves, as well as the detail of the modelled blouse upper parts, there are no doubts, that all these doll heads and others, which are shown on the following pages, were produced from the above named company.

Full view of the doll pictured on the opposite page,　the beautiful profile ...

... and the rear of the head with the blue shawl.

Shoulder head made from parian in the Meissen-Genre - the blond painted hair style is identical with the front of the doll pictured on page 81, only the rear of the head has been remodelled and adorned with a blue shawl with gold patterns. The modelling of the rose (partially damaged), harebells and leaves can be recognized here rather clearly, because this head is larger, the painting and modelling is identical with that of the doll on page 81 - 3 sewing holes in front and behind - cloth body with forearms made from parian - 23 3/4in (60 cm) large - approx. 1875.

Almost identical shoulder head like the one pictured on page 87, only here with 3 modelled roses instead of with one.

Full view of the doll pictured on the opposite page - (arms are included).

The rear of the head of the doll pictured on the opposite page with the fine details of the painting and modelling.

Shoulder head made from Parian - brown painted curled hair style with decorations in the Meissen-Genre, modelled rose (slightly damaged) and leaves, the painting is identical to the dolls shown on page 81, 83 and 85 - cloth body with forearms made from Parian - 17in (43 cm) large - approx. 1870.

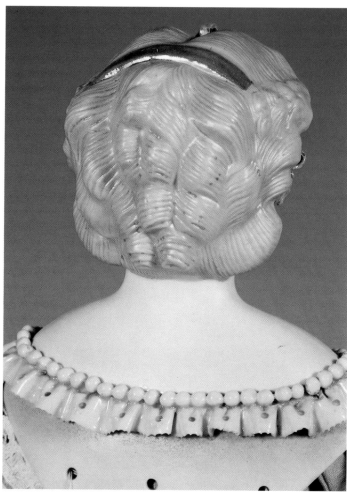

Profile, rear of the head and inside of the head with inscription of the doll pictured on the opposite page.

Inscription in the interior of the head: Bought Christmas - Dec 25 - year 1871 for Adeline Meyer aged six years then .... 1929 .... 64 ....1865. Bought by Mrs. Fred Distelbusch, 48 Devoe ...., Williamsburg.

Shoulder head made from Parian - the blond painted hair style with forehead curls is with 3 modelled gold-pink colored bows, the modelled blouse upper part decorated with an edge of modelled pearls - blue glass eyes - cloth body - 22 1/2in (57 cm) large - 1865.

Rear of the head and full view of the
doll pictured on the opposite page.

Shoulder head made from very pale tinted bisque in the Meissen-Genre - modelled, combed to the rear hair style with modelled black hair band, with gold and painted white dots, adorned at the side with a pink, gold bow- modelled blouse upper part with modelled rose and frills - blue glass eyes - 3 sewing holes in front and behind - cloth body with forearms made from bisque - 16 1/2in (42 cm) large - approx. 1875.

1. Shoulder head made from china with modelled blouse upper part and glazed bow - hair style and rear of the head are identical with Fig. 2 and 5 - size of the head 4in (10 cm) - approx. 1860.

2. Shoulder head made from parian - type Empress Eugénie - similar hair style, see Fig. 7 - modelled blouse upper part with glazed collar and bow - cloth body with leather arms - 19 3/4in (50 cm) large - approx. 1865.

3. Male shoulder head made from bisque - identical with the face on page 93, only the modelling of the hair style (brown) and the shirt was changed- cloth body with leather arms - 24in (61 cm) large - glazed collar and bow.

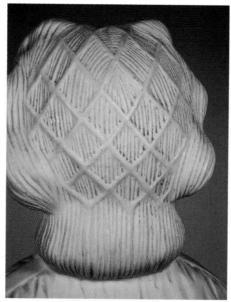

4. + 5. The rear of the head of the doll in Fig. 1 with hair-net, which is identical with the one in Fig. 5.

6. Rear of the head of the doll pictured on the opposite page.

7. Drawing of the Empress Eugénie, which shows clearly the hair combed to the rear, as shown with the dolls in Fig. 1 and 2.

Dresden Gentleman

Shoulder head made from parian - modelled blond painted curled hair style of a young cavalier - this doll is known under the name of "Dresden Gentleman" or only in short "Dresden Gent" in America - modelled dress shirt with painted and glazed bow - two sewing holes in front and behind - 15 3/4in (40 cm) large - approx. 1865.
Similar heads were made from china and bisque, with black painted hair and glass eyes. Also this doll has been associated, due to identical modelling and painting (see closely all bows), to the above indicated company.

Shoulder head made from parian - the brown hair style is nearly identical in front to that of the doll pictured on page 92 (Fig. 2), however with modelled pearls, without modelled upper blouse and the rear of the head has been remodelled - 6 1/2in (16 cm) large - around 1870. A large head with sharp contours.

Full view of the doll pictured on the opposite page.

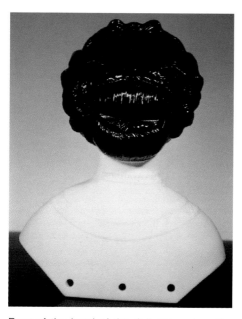

Rear of the head of the doll pictured above.

Similar shoulder head made from parian as above on the left, also the rear of the head is identical - size 15in (38 cm) - approx. 1870. A small head with flat contours.

Rear of the head of the doll pictured on the opposite page.

Countess Dagmar«

Shoulder head made from parian - named "Countess Dagmar" - painted black hair style with modelled bow on the head and modelled blouse upper part - identical doll heads are also found with blond or brown painted hair style- three sewing holes in front and behind - cloth body with old forearms made from china (latter was added on later) - size 19in (48 cm) - approx. 1865.

Two doll heads, which clearly originated from the same model, on the left a swivel neck head made from Parian, on the right a shoulder head made from bisque, which was produced several years later, around 1890, because it already has an open mouth with teeth, while the other head still displays a closed mouth - both doll heads have identical blue glass eyes and the identical hair styles, but the rear of the head on the right is decorated with modelled roses and leaves. Because of the similarities of the faces, the identical modelling and painting both heads are attributed to the above named company.

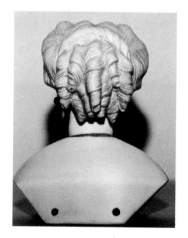
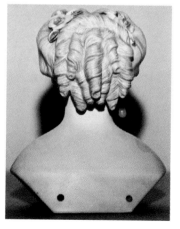

Shoulder head made from bisque, which was modelled with longish curled hair style painted light brown - blue glass eyes - cloth body with leather arms - 17 3/4in (45 cm) large - approx. 1880. Modelling and painting is attributed likewise to the company Dornheim, Koch & Fischer. Full view of the doll can be seen on page 99.

Shoulder head made from bisque with light brown painted hair style and modelled blouse upper part with glazed frills and bow - markings: 9 - painted blue eyes - cloth body with leather arms - 24in (61 cm) large - approx. 1880. Due to the painting and modelling this head is attributed to the above-mentioned company.

Full view of the doll pictured below.

Full view of the doll described on page 97.

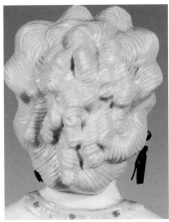

Rear of the heads of both dolls pictured above.

Shoulder head made from bisque identical to the one pictured on the opposite, this time with glass eyes - cloth body - 14in (36 cm) large - approx. 1875.

 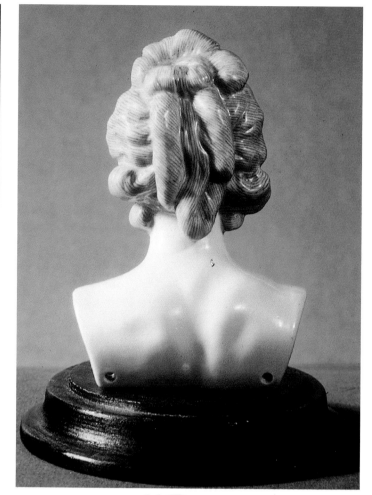

Shoulder head of white china lightly blushed with pink in cleavage and at base of throat. Extravagant light brown hairstyle accented with brown strokes. Blue hair band edged with gold. Carved blue intaglio eyes, molded upper and lower lids with dark eyeliner and pale orange accent line above and even paler, very fine orange line below the eye. Painted upper and lower lashes. Brush-stroked eyebrows match the hair. Shaded lips with darker line between. 4 1/4in (11 cm) circa 1890.

The back of the doll head on the right with the beautiful modelled back.

The doll heads presented here on both pages are not marked, however others were found with identical faces and similarities in the modelling and painting, which have a marking, a bishops staff (see below), on the inside of the shoulder plate, which belongs to the above named company.

A side view of the doll (see page 101), which shows the double chin, which corresponded to the ideals of that period.

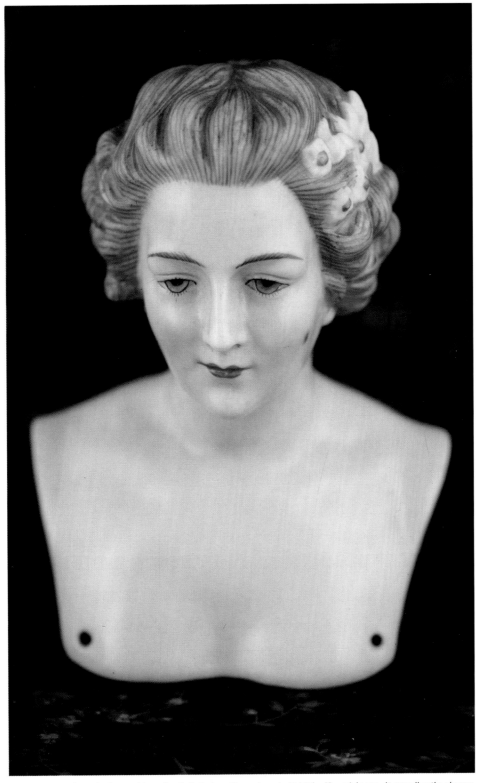

Shoulder head made from china, flesh tinted - although only 3 1/2in (9 cm) large, it excellently shows the anatomical details, like breasts and shoulder-blades - especially the detailed painting: the skillful hair style was painted in light beige with brown lines and trimmed with blossoms - blue intaglio eyes with modelled upper and lower eyelids, red eyelid strokes and painted eyelashes - the shoulder plate dabbed with pink shadings - approx. 1890.

Shoulder head made from china, white skin color, inside also glazed - black painted hair style - 6 3/4in (17 cm) large - approx. 1870.
The rear of the head displays the identical modelling of the hair style, as is shown below on the right.

Dolls with the flat hair style are called in America "flat top".

On the opposite page, top left, a broken doll head is shown, which was found on the land of the above indicated company. Because of the similarities of the faces as well as in the modelling and painting (under consideration, that the models were often altered), all three doll heads presented here are   attributed to this company.

Shoulder head made from china, white skin color - black painted hair style (necklace not modelled) - 6in (15 cm) high - approx. 1870.

Rear of the head of the above pictured doll, which is identical with the rear of the head of the doll pictured on page 103.

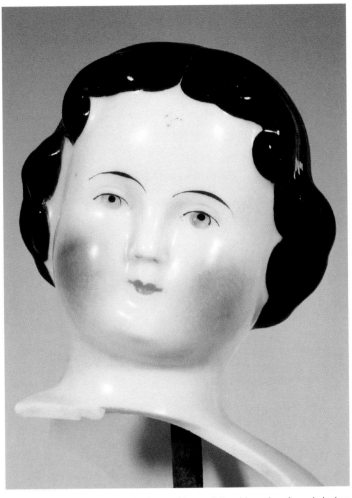

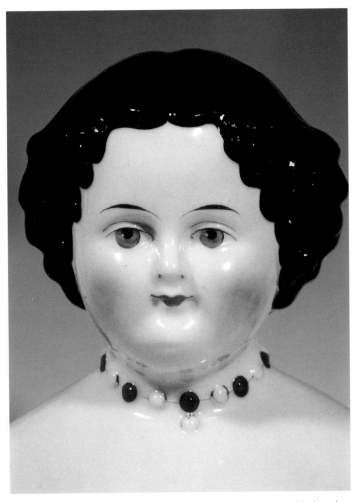

Broken shoulder head made from china, white skin color, found during excavation on the land of the above named company - black painted hair style - size 4 3/4in (12 cm) - approx. 1875.

Shoulder head made from china, white skin color, black painted hair style - painted blue eyes - modelled necklace - size 4 3/4in (12 cm) - approx. 1870.

Rear of the head of the above pictured head.

Very small shoulder head made from china with simple painting, found likewise on the land of the above-mentioned company.

Small doll - shoulder head made from china with simple painting - leather body - 10in (25 cm) large - around 1900.

Dolly Madison

Shoulder head made from bisque - blond hair style with modelled dark blue hairband and bow - painted necklace with pendant, lightly modelled blouse upper part - cobalt blue glass eyes - pierced ears - cloth body with forearms made from bisque - 15in (38 cm) large - approx. 1880.

Shoulder head made from parian - called in America "Dolly Madison" - blond hair style with modelled dark blue hairband - cobalt blue glass eyes - a very popular doll type, which is also found in china and bisque with painted eyes and black hair.

Rear of the head of the above pictured doll.

Front and back of a raw model. In front over the forehead are the modelled snail shaped curls, the modelled band and bow as well as the ears are clearly recognizable.
This raw model was found on the land of the above named company, and is identical with the doll pictured on the opposite page.

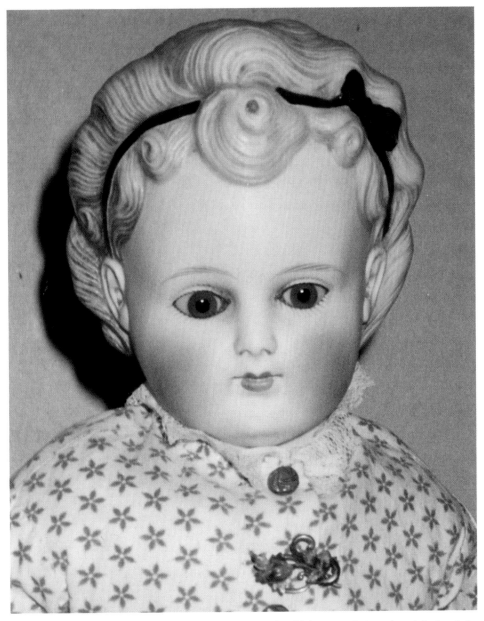

Shoulder head made from parian - blond painted hair style with large snail shaped modelled curls in the middle of the forehead and with modelled black band with a bow on the side - cobalt blue glass eyes - cloth body with forearms made from parian - 21in (53 cm) large - around 1870.
Face and modelling of the hair style, the band, the bow and the ears are identical to the raw model pictured on the opposite page. No doubt exists, that this and both doll heads pictured on the opposite page were produced by above-mentioned company.

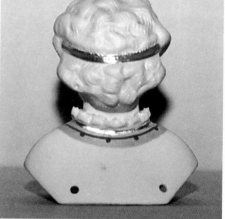

Pictured above: Shoulder head made from bisque - blond painted hair style with dark blue bow - painted eyes - leather body with forearms made from bisque - 12 1/2in (32 cm) large - approx. 1880.

If one were to compare this doll with the ones found on the pages 104 and 105, the different criteria, e.g. similarities of the face, the modelling and painting (color of the hair band) points to the same company as named above.

Pictured above right: Full view of the doll pictured on the left.

Pictured above and left: The rear of the head of the doll pictured above on the left is largely similar to the rear of the head of the doll pictured on the opposite page.

Shoulder head made from parian - blond painted hair style with modelled hairband with bow - painted eyes - modelled and decorated frills and beautifully painted blouse upper part - apparently this doll head is a luxury version to the ones pictured on pages 104, 105 and 106 - approx. 1875.

Shoulder head made from parian with blond painted hair style, modelled hair clasp and necklace with pendant - cobalt blue glass eyes - leather body with arms made from composition - 17 1/2in (44 cm) large - ca.1875.

Pictured above: Profile of the doll on the left.
Pictured in the middle: View of the doll on the right.

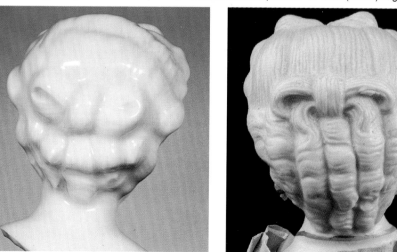

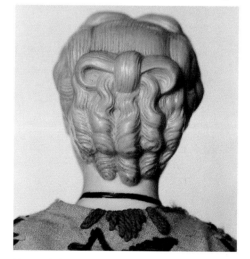

Glazed raw model, whose modelling (considerating the changes) points to the above-mentioned company.

Rear of the head of the above pictured doll.

Rear of the head of the doll pictured on the opposite page.

Shoulder head made from parian with strongly modelled dark blonde painted hair style - modelled comb, necklace and pendant - cobalt blue glass eyes - pierced ears - leather body with wedges at hips and legs, leather arms, hands with individually sewn fingers - 20in (51 cm) large - approx. 1870. Although the face has hardly any similarities to the doll pictured on the opposite page, the rear of the heads show, that both were made from the same mold. Both doll heads due to the similarities in the modelling and painting were attributed to the above named company.

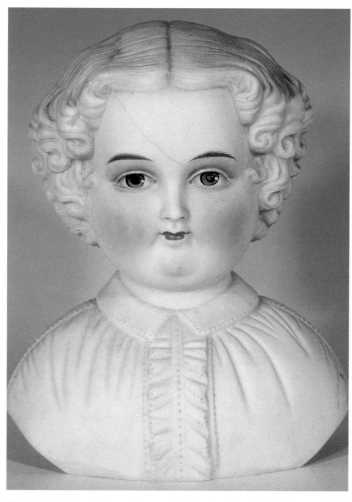 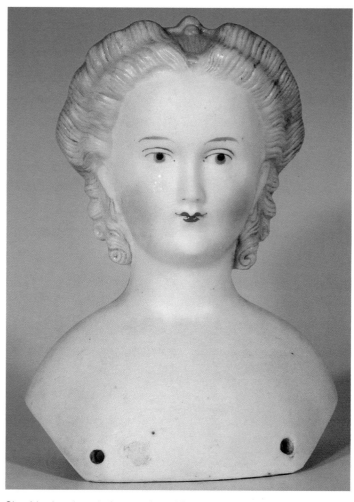

Shoulder head made from bisque with blond painted hair style - modelled blouse upper part - painted intaglio eyes with painted eyelashes and eyelid strokes - size 4 3/4in (12 cm) - approx. 1880.

Shoulder head made from parian with blond painted hair style - painted eyes - size 4in (10 cm) - approx. 1875.

 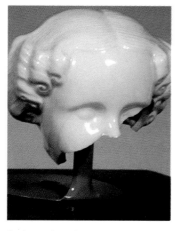 

Profile of the doll head above.

Broken glazed raw model, whose hair style is identical with that of the doll above.

Raw models (on the right glazed), found on the land of the above named company.

Shoulder head made from bisque with blond painted hair style - painted eyes - approx. 1880, attributed to the above-mentioned company.
If one compares this and the doll head on the left page (above on the right) with the raw models below it, it becomes obvious, that there are similarities in the modelling of the hair styles. Also there are similarities in the painting.

Marking: 3 104 Germany   *»Pet Name«*

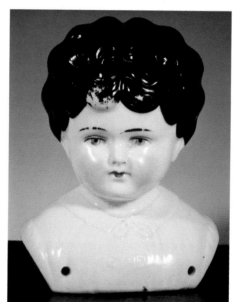

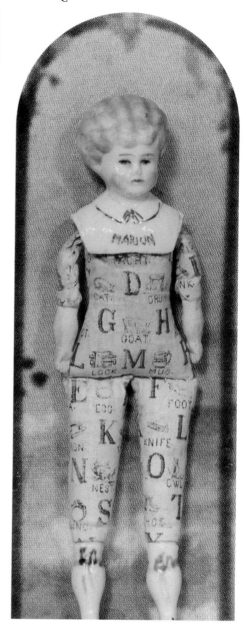

Picture above left: Shoulder head made from bisque with blossom shaped modelled hat and blouse upper part - markings: 3 104 Germany - painted eyes - 3in (8 cm) large - around 1900.

Heads with blossom shaped modelled hats, which were also called "Marguerite Dolls" (see also page 183), were exported above all to America.

Picture above middle: The rear view of the doll's head.

Picture on the right: Shoulder head made from china with simple hair style and modelled blouse upper part - markings (in front): "Ethel", at the rear: PATENT APP'D FOR // Germany - painted eyes - 6in (15 cm) large - approx. 1895.
These doll heads, which were also called "Pet name", were also found with blond colored hair and with many other names, e.g.: Agnes, Bertha, Daisy, Dorothy, Edith, Esther, Ethel, Florence, Helen, Mabel, Marion, Pauline etc..

Shoulder head made from china with modelled blouse upper part, on the front side the name Marion in gold letters is found, on the rear stands PATENT APP'D FOR // GERMANY - painted eyes - original cloth body with letters - 7 1/2in (19 cm) large - approx. 1895.

Marking: W

Shoulder head made from bisque - blond painted hair style with modelled cap with Pompons - markings: W - painted blue eyes - closed mouth - leather body - 24 3/4in (63 cm) large - approx. 1890.

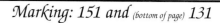

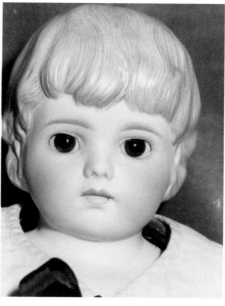

Shoulder head made from bisque - blond painted hair style with modelled black comb - markings: 128 - pierced ears - leather body - 17 1/2in (44 cm) large - approx. 1885.

Childlike shoulder head made from bisque with blond painted short hairstyle - brown glass eyes - ears not pierced - leather body with arms made from composition - 23 3/4in (60 cm) large - approx. 1880.

Identical doll pictured on the opposite page - markings: 151 - visible the modelled blouse upper part and the beautiful forearms made from bisque.

The rear of the head of the above doll.

Three shoulder heads made from light bisque - the doll in the middle has blue, the one on the right brown glass eyes and a leather body with composition arms - the same dolls (like the one pictured on the opposite page) are known with the mold number 131 - all are from approx. 1880.

Marking: 151

Shoulder head made from bisque with modelled blouse upper part - markings: 151 - blue glass eyes - leather body with forearms made from bisque - 16 1/2in (42 cm) large - approx. 1880.
This doll was the most beautiful face, which the company Kling created and it came in different variations with different hair styles and decorations on to the market, see also page 114, upper row, as well as the pages 116, 117 and 119.

Marking: 141

Marking: 135

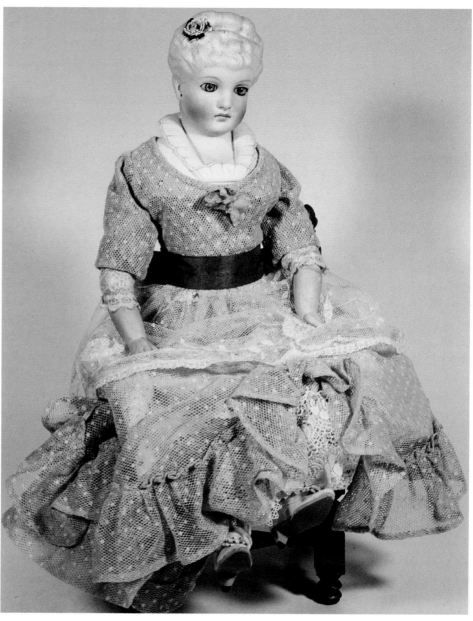

Shoulder head made from bisque, the modelled blond hair style is adorned with modelled feather and comb - markings: 141.

Full view of the doll pictured on the opposite page.

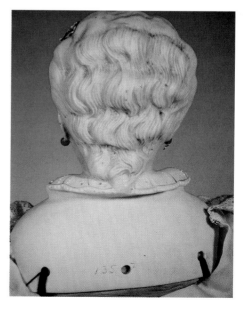

Side and rear of the head of the doll pictured on the opposite page with the shoulder plate and the markings.

Marking: 135 7

Shoulder head made from bisque with blond painted hair style and modelled rose and leaves (damaged), the collar with modelled dots and light blue lines   markings: 135 7 - blue glass eyes with paperweight effect - leather body with forearms made from bisque - 19in (48 cm) large - approx. 1880.

Markings: 141 2, lower row: 185 6 and 87 295

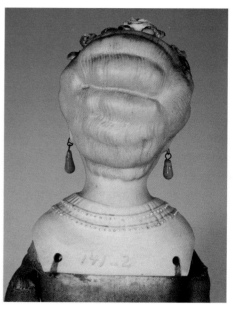

The rear of the head of the doll pictured on the opposite page with the shoulder plate and markings.

Picture on the left: Full view of the doll pictured on the opposite page and the "Dresden Gentleman", which is described on page 93.

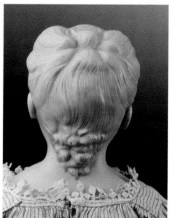

Shoulder head made from bisque with blond painted braided hair style - markings: 185 6 - painted blue eyes - cloth body - 20 1/2in (52 cm) large - around 1880.

The side of the doll on the left.

Shoulder head made from bisque - markings: 87 295 - blue glass eyes - leather body with bisque forearms - 24in (61 cm) large - approx. 1885.

The rear of the head of the doll on the left.

Marking: 141 2

Shoulder head made from bisque with blond painted hair style and modelled flowers and leaves (damaged and repaired) and modelled blouse upper part - markings: 141 2 - brown glass eyes - cloth body with forearms and legs made from bisque - 14in (36 cm) large - approx. 1880.

Markings: Blue Eagle, Red Apple, with S and KPM

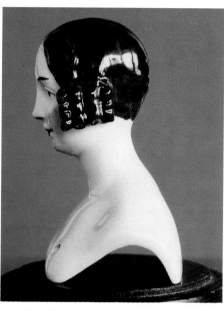

1. Shoulder head made from pale pink tinted china - marks in the inside of the shoulder (see Fig. 4 and 5) - the hair was painted in various different brown tones, at the sides curls and at the rear of the head a flat hair knot - 3 1/2in (9.5 cm) large - approx. 1850.

2. and 3. The classic profiles of the doll heads pictured here, show that they have identical faces and that the hair was modelled differently.

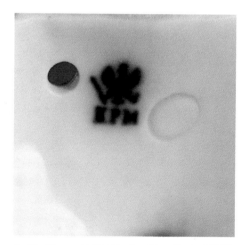

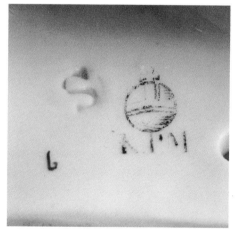

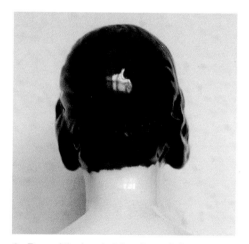

4. Markings of KPM Berlin: Blue Eagle "KPM".

5. Markings of KPM Berlin: "S" red apple "KPM" and red hook.

6. Rear of the head of the above doll.

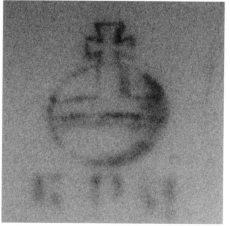

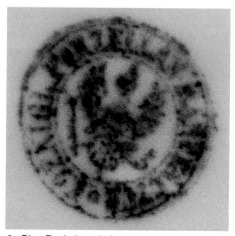

7. Markings of the doll pictured on the opposite page: Red Apple KPM.

8. Blue Eagle in a circle.

Marking: Red Apple KPM and Blue Eagle in a Circle and 9

Shoulder head made from glazed pink tinted china with long neck - markings in the inside of the front shoulder plate: Red Apple with KPM (Fig. 7) and in the inside of the back shoulder plate: Blue Eagle (Fig. 8) and the numeral 9 - hair painted in various brown tones, at the rear of the head a flat modelled hair knot - lightly smiling closed mouth with dark red middle line - painted blue eyes with pointed painted eye line and modelled eyelids - the head is 6 1/2in (16.5 cm) large - approx. 1850.

Morning Glory   *Marking: 54 , stamped Scepter, 7 a*

A simpler, smaller version of the "Morning Glory" in profile and from the side - no markings - cloth body - 14 1/2in (37 cm) large - approx. 1860.

Profile of the "Morning Glory" described on the opposite page with its beautiful flower decoration. Since these extraordinary dolls are very rare, it will interest the collector, to see the exact detail. If one compares the picture on the right, which is somewhat smaller, with the one on the left, one can recognize clearly the quality differences. On the right the simple model with molded flowers, on the right the first-class quality with modelled flowers. The painting is far more simpler with the doll on the right but still of course artistically.

Morning Glory   *Marking: 54 , stamped Scepter, 7 a*

Pictures above and below: Rear and front view of the head of the "Morning Glory".

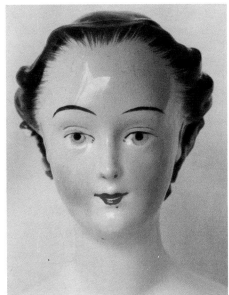

Shoulder head made from pink tinted china (shading clearly visible at the edges of the shoulder plate) - markings at the lower back of the shoulder plate: 54 stamped scepter 7 a (picture below on the right), inside a sign in red color - brown and black painted hair style with modelled flowers, because of this flower, this doll is called in America the "Morning Glory", in Germany this flower is called the "cone flower" (Ipomoea) - painted eyes with modelled eyelids - long neck and modelled breasts - 7in (17.5 cm) large - approx. 1850.
This head belongs to the most beautiful doll heads, which were manufactured in china.

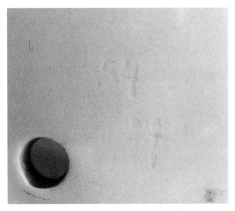

The marking with the stamped scepter and 54.

Morning Glory Marking : S 63

Shoulder head made from flesh tinted china - "Morning Glory" - markings on the inside of the right shoulder: S 63 (identical S like in Fig. 5, page 120) - black painted hair style - painted blue eyes - long neck and modelled breast - three sewing holes in front and back - size of the head 7in (17.5 cm) - cloth body with leather arms and boots - total size: 26in (66 cm) - approx. 1860.

The marking of this "Morning Glory".

Marking: KPM and Scepter

Pictures on the left and below on the right: Shoulder head made from pink china - simple brown painted hair style with hair knots at the back of the head - markings: "KPM" and scepter - painted blue eyes with modelled eyelids, red eye strokes, however no eyelid strokes - leather body - 17 1/2in (44 cm) large - approx. 1850.

Pictures in the middle and above on the right: Shoulder head made from pink china - simple brown painted hair style - markings on the inside of the shoulder plate: "KPM" as well as the green scepter - painted blue eyes with modelled eyelids, red eye strokes, however no eyelid strokes - leather body with wooden arms and legs - 16 1/2in (42 cm) large - around 1850.

Marking: Crossed Swords

Full view of a Meissen doll described on the opposite page.

Marking: Crossed Swords

Shoulder head made from china of simple, classic beauty with longish nose and long neck - markings on the inside of the shoulder plate: 66 7 V 702 5, crossed swords - white skin color - light brown painted hair style, brown streaks, with a hair knot at the back of the head - painted brown eyes - cloth body with forearms and legs made from china - 15 1/2in (39 cm) large - approx. 1840.

Marking: Diamond shaped Shield

Dolls made from Nymphenburg China

With a wealth of ideas and events the Bavarian arts and crafts society celebrated in 1901, its 50 years of existence. In the courtyard of the Artist house in Munich, an anniversary market was held with works made by the society members.

Between the sales stands there was a doll booth named "Nora" (jokingly after Ibsens drama "A Doll Home"), where lady dolls made from Nymphenburg china were sold. A member had displaced at its disposal a "bride" clothed, South German manger figure from the 18th Century, which had been modelled in china. (This figure with its painted wax head, cloth body and wooden hands and feet was acquired later by the Munich City museum (see lower page 129, middle figure). The china head and limbs are exactly one seventh smaller than the original model, around which the ceramic mass shrinks when fired.

As the party organizer, the architect

Gabriel von Seidl had bought about 50 sets of dolls from the commercial minister Albert Bäuml, who was the tenant of the Royal China Manufacture Nymphenburg. In the arts and crafts company Steinicken & Lohr, he had cloth bodies produced. Then he sent the naked dolls to various ladies of Munichs society with the request for them to dress them. A delightful diversity from Rokoko to Biedermeier ladies or mondane modern were returned (see below on the right).

The china manufacture Nymphenburg continued to produce small orders of dolls up to the 1st World War.

The immovable shoulder heads have a peculiar modelled hair style, high forehead with downward looking eyes and a touch of an amusing smile around the mouth. The hands are very graceful; the feet have brown soles and blue sandal strappings painted on (exactly like the manger figure). However there are also copies with black, painted on

shoes. The heads are marked on the inside of the shoulder plate with the Nymphenburg diamond shaped blind tooling, over this a star. Annoyingly this marking points to the year of manufacture 1850-62, however one knows, that around 1900 under Albert Bäuml this marking was occasionally used as well.

Since 1990 the Royal China Manufacture Nymphenburg manufactures this doll exactly as the original. Further it offers a historic Lady doll type with upright braided hair style (see below on the left, top picture), as well as two different child heads with bonnets and with painted hair (see on the left, bottom picture) and baby limbs. These new series of dolls have a green glazed stamp: the diamond shaped shield and an "A" (for the Duke Albrecht, the head of the House of Wittelsbach).

Marking: Diamond shaped Shield

Three shoulder heads made from glazed china. They had and always have the identical size, in 3 1/2in (9 cm). The hair styles can always look a little differently, since the heads are reworked with the modelling tools and are then painted by hand - cloth body - approx. 1905.

Two dolls of the Nymphenburg manufacture from 1901, as they are manufactured today. In the middle the manger figure from the 18th Century, which served as model.

Irish Queen Marking: 8552

Porcelain Factory Limbach
Shoulder head made from parian with extravagant black painted hair style with bow, modelled blouse with upright collar - markings at the back of the shoulder plate: 8552 with clover leaf - painted intaglio eyes - open-closed mouth with modelled teeth - approx. 1875 - in America this doll is called the "Irish Queen".

Porcelain Factory Rudolstadt-Volkstedt
Shoulder head made from parian with simple blond hair style and modelled bonnet - painted eyes - 11 3/4in (30 cm) large - approx. 1890.

Shoulder head made from stone bisque with brown streaked hair style and modelled hat with painted flowers - painted blue eyes - wax cloth body with celluloid forearms - 13in (33 cm) large - around 1900.

The glazed raw model with the triangular shaped bonnet, the bow under the chin and the hair style is identical with the doll pictured above.

Identical raw model with the head pictured above; only the flowers on the bonnet are not modelled but painted. The cording on the back (both Figures below) is however identical.

A doll with the head made by the porcelain factory Limbach (see also opposite page, picture above on the right) before the background photograph of a child from around the turn of the Century.

Shoulder head made from parian, which is pictured here as an interesting comparison with the head pictured on the opposite page. This head has for instance a round face, while the head on the opposite page displays an almost angular face, the hair style was remodelled with a point in the middle of the forehead and at the side wide curls, also the back of the head was changed, up to the middle it is first wavy and then has modelled curls, which flow around to the back of the head, the bow is located far more deeper at the rear of the head.

Full view of the doll on the opposite page in a reproduced dress made from old material with rich hand embroidery, below the rear of the head of the same doll.

Marking: S. 12. H.

Shoulder head made from parian with brown painted hair style, modelled curls down to the shoulders and a modelled black bow - markings at the edge of the front shoulder plate: S 12 H - light blue glass eyes with shiny iris - wire eyelets, which stand out from the earlobes, to attach earrings to (are not known with dolls of other companies) - the dividing line of the closed mouth is painted in the middle with a jagged edge - leather body with bisque forearms - 25 1/2in (65 cm) large - approx. 1875.

Among the early doll heads produced by the above-mentioned company, this model is relatively frequent. There are many variations known e.g. with painted eyes, as swivel breast plate head, with modelled necklace with cross, with different hair styles, in blond, also in bisque and later as a swivel head for composition bodies with wig made under the mold number 719.

Marking: S 10 H

Shoulder head made from parian - markings: S 10 H - approx. 1875 - the face, bow and hair style point out, that one is dealing here with a variation of the same model head, only this time with painted eyes, from which also the dolls on pages 132 and 133 come from.

Bottom row:
These dolls are attributed to the company Simon & Halbig, because the modelling and painting point to it.

Marking: S. 12. H.

Shoulder head made from bisque - markings: S 12 H - brown glass eyes - fine painting and modelling - closed mouth with contour - leather bodies - 23 3/4in (60 cm) large - approx. 1885.

Shoulder head made from china - black painted hair style - painted blue eyes, strong red cheeks - cloth body with bisque forearms and cloth legs - approx. 1865.

Profile and rear of the head of the doll on the left.

Shoulder head made from china - black painted hair style - painted eyes - cloth body with china arms and legs - 21 1/2in (54 cm) large - approx. 1870.

The rear of the head of the doll with the hair-net. This and the doll on the right were manufactured probably by Hertel, Schwab & Co ..

Shoulder head made from china - black painted hair style - painted blue eyes - cloth body with china arms and cloth legs - 16 1/2in (42 cm) large - approx. 1865.

The rear of the head with modelled, black painted bow.

Shoulder head made from china - black painted hair style with red hair band - painted eyes - cloth body with bisque arms, legs with knee joints made from leather - 17 3/4in (45 cm) large - approx. 1865.

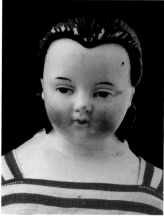

The profile of the doll.

The rear of the head with corkscrew curls and the red hair band.

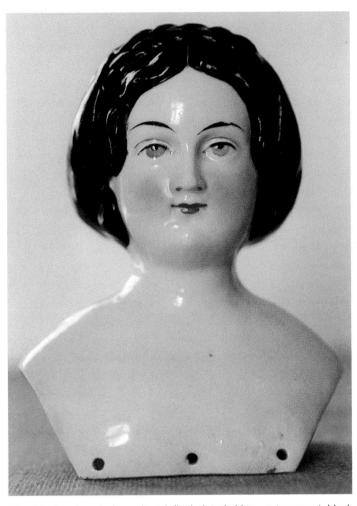

Shoulder head made from glazed, flesh tinted china - extravagant, black painted hair style - markings on the inside of the breast plate: 7, with black ink 117, engraved 115 - painted blue eyes - 5 1/2in (14 cm) large - approx. 1865.

Shoulder head made from glazed china, skin color white - painted black hair style with middle parting and curls - cloth body with wine red leather forearms and stepped fingers - 21 1/2 (54 cm) large - approx. 1865. Most likely made by Alt, Beck & Gottschalck.

The profile of the doll above.

Full view of the doll above.

Shoulder head made from china with skillfully modelled, black painted hair style with corkscrew curls, modelled hair band with bow at the rear of the head, tassle and hair-net - painted blue eyes - cloth body with leather arms - 20 3/4in (53 cm) large - approx. 1870.

Shoulder head made from china, identical model like the doll on the left - cloth body with forearms and legs made from china - 23in (58 cm) - approx. 1870.

The rear of the head of the doll above shows clearly the modelling of the tassles and the hair-net.

Spill Curls

Curly Top

Shoulder head made from china with modelled, falling, light brown painted curls - modelled black hair band - painted blue eyes - cloth body - 15in (38 cm) large - approx. 1875 - in America these doll heads with this type of hair style are called "Spill Curls".

Shoulder head made from china with curl hair style painted in "milk coffee" color - painted eyes - cloth body - 19 3/4in (50 cm) large - approx. 1875 - in America known as "Curly Top" - also found with black hair color in parian and bisque.

Shoulder head made from china - markings: "Germany" - white skin color - the curly hair style is painted only in the valleys of the modelling in light brown - blue painted eyes - two sewing holes in front and behind - 11in (28 cm) - around 1900.

Picture on the left: Reflection with back of head.

Shoulder head made from china with extravagant black painted hair style - forearms and legs made from china, the latter with modelled boots with heels - 27 1/2in (70 cm) large - approx. 1870.

Shoulder head made from china with black painted hair style - painted eyes - leather body - 27 1/2in (70 cm) large - approx. 1865.
Similarities with the dolls on pages 102 and 103 point to Hertel, Schwab & Co. as the producers.

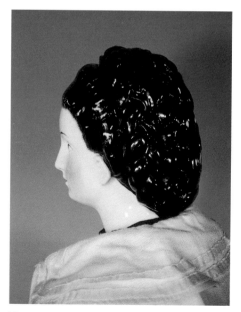

The profile of the above doll.

The rear of the head of the above doll with the beautifully modelled corkscrew curls.

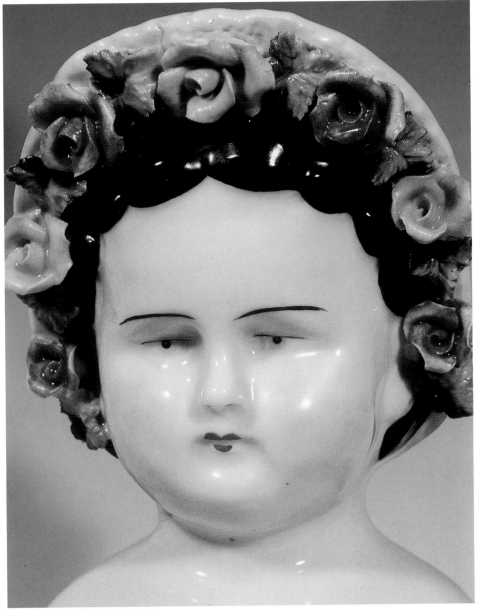

Full view of the doll on the left.

Shoulder head made from glazed china, white skin color - very extravagant modelled bonnet with roses, the back only white - in comparison poor painting - cloth body with forearms made from china - 19in (48 cm) large - approx. 1890.

Shoulder head made from glazed china with modelled bonnet, with painted flowers - painted eyes - closed mouth - leather body - 13in (33 cm) large - around 1890.

Marking: 5 A 5

The rear of the head of the doll with the beautiful modelled throat frill and the ornament comb.

On the pages 142 to 155 a series of outstanding doll heads are presented, which belong to the most exquisite, created in this area. They have been marked usually with letters and numbers, not all were marked and all display similarities in the painting. Nearly all of the doll heads presented here in this book with painted eyes have the same painted dots at the identical place and the eyebrows are done in a non-stop stroke, while the heads with glass eyes have painted stroked eyebrows. (One is always dealing with the same type of glass eye.) The exquisite painted mouth has a wavy contour and a dark red dividing line. Some of the following criteria point to the large toys and porcellain company J.D. Kestner Jr., although this hypothesis could not be documented, one knows that Kestner advertised e.g. china and bisque heads with modelled hair, which until today could not however be identified. Kestner marked his doll heads - if at all - before 1900 with letters and numbers, known as the Kestner Alphabet.

Kestner belonged to those porcelain companies, that created the most outstanding doll heads. It is not to be assumed, that these heads were manufactured by a small insignificant porcelain factory. Most of these doll heads presented here originated from the Borgfeldt Collection.

Shoulder head made from bisque with blond painted hair style and modelled ornament comb and extravagantly painted blouse upper part with modelled collars, frills and bow - markings: 5 A 5 - blue glass eyes with shiny irises - feathery eyebrows, closed mouth with contour and dark red dividing line - 5in (13 cm) large - approx. 1880.

Marking: *5 C.5.*

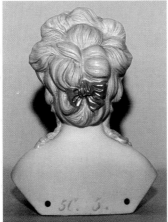

The rear of the head of the doll on the left with the gold-red bow and the marking.

Shoulder head made from bisque with blond painted hair style with very beautifully modelled curls and modelled gold colored star - markings: 5 C 5 - feathery eyebrows, blue glass eyes with shiny irises - closed mouth with projecting modelled upper lip, dark red dividing line and contour - 4 3/4in (12.5 cm) large - approx. 1880.

Marking: 5 E

Shoulder head made from bisque with black painted hair style and modelled red bonnet with gold edge as well as three rowed gold colored necklace, at the rear of the head long modelled curls and one modelled strain with tassles - markings at the lower edge of the back shoulder plate: 5 E - painted eyes, eyebrows in a nonstop stroke - closed mouth with contour and dark red dividing line - 4in (10 cm) large - around 1885.

This and the head on the opposite page were produced possibly for the international doll series, which showed the dolls in costumes from different countries, produced for the Import House Butler Bros..

Marking: 2 K 3

Shoulder head made from bisque with blond painted hair style and modelled costume hood, three rowed gold colored necklace and blouse upper part with bows - markings: 2 K 3 - painted eyes, eyebrows in a nonstop stroke - closed mouth with contour and dark red dividing line - 4in (10 cm) large - around 1885.

Marking: 3 𝓛 5

Full view of the doll with forearms made from bisque. It is wearing an extravagantly worked dress, in which it won the first prize at an exhibition.

Shoulder head made from bisque with blond painted hair style and modelled band in blue and gold color - markings: 3 L 5 - necklace not modelled - blue glass eyes with shiny irises, feathery eyebrows - closed mouth with contour and dark red dividing line - approx. 1885.

The rear of the head with the beautifully modelled hair style.

Marking: 5 H 5

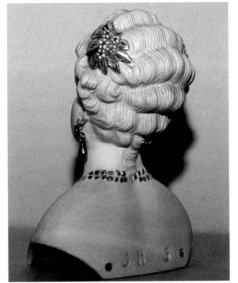

The rear of the head with the marking.

Shoulder head made from bisque with blond painted hair style and modelled white blossoms and gold-green leaves as well as a three rowed gold colored necklace - markings: 5 H 5 or 3 H 5 - blue glass eyes with shiny irises and feathery eyebrows - closed mouth with contour and dark red dividing line - 5in (13 cm) large - approx. 1880.

Marking: 4.N°9

Profile and rear of the head of the doll on the right.

Full view of the same doll, well visible the beautiful old bisque arms - the dress was reworked from an original dress out of that period using old material (silk and tull).

Marking: 4 N 9

Shoulder head made from light tinted bisque with modelled necklace and medallion - markings: 4 N 9 - blond painted, especially extravagant modelled hair style with long shoulder curls - blue painted eyes, eyebrows painted in one stroke - closed mouth with contour and dark red dividing line - cloth body with forearms made from bisque - lower legs made from red material with sewn on black leather boots with heels - 21 3/4in (55 cm) large - approx. 1870.

Marking: 5M5

Shoulder head made from bisque - markings: 5 M 5 - blond painted hair style - very beautifully modelled and painted collar with bow - painted blue eyes, eyebrows painted on one line - closed mouth with contour and dark red dividing line - 4 1/2in (11 cm) large - approx. 1885.

Marking: 4R7.

The rear of the head of the doll with the modelled frills and the well recognizable marking.

Shoulder head made from bisque - markings: 4 R 7 - dark blond painted hair style - extravagant painted blouse upper part with modelled frills and bow - painted blue eyes, eyebrows painted on one line - closed mouth with contour and dark red dividing line - cloth body with arms and legs made fom cloth, partially made from leathers - 19in (48 cm) large - approx. 1880.

Marking: 5 U 2

Shoulder head made from bisque, modelled bonnet with frill, above and under the chin a bow in red and gold - markings: 5 U 2
- painted blue eyes, eyebrows in a painted nonstop line - closed mouth with contour and dark red dividing line - 4in (10 cm) large
- approx. 1885.

Marking: 5√2

Shoulder head made from bisque with blond painted hair and modelled bonnet with feathers and cockade - markings: 5 V 2 - blue glass eyes with shiny irises, painted feathery eyebrows - closed mouth with contour and dark red dividing line - 4 3/4in (12 cm) large - approx. 1885.

Shoulder head with blond painted hair style and modelled gold pearl jewelry - without markings - blue glass eyes with shiny irises and painted feathery eyebrows - closed mouth with contour and dark red dividing line - 4 3/4in (12.5 cm) large - approx. 1880. Although this head has no markings, the modelling and painting point to the same producer, presumably Kestner, who also created the other doll heads (see pages 142 to 153).

Shoulder head made from bisque with painted middle brown hair style and modelled bonnet with flower trimmings and bow - painted eyes - leather body - 17 3/4in (45 cm) large - approx. 1885.
Although this head has no markings, the modelling and painting point to the same producer, presumably Kestner, who also created the other doll heads (see pages 142 to 153).

Shoulder head made from bisque with blond painted hair style and modelled blouse upper part with frills and bow - painted eyes - pierced ears with wire eyelets (latter up until now only found with the company Simon & Halbig) - approx. 1885.

Shoulder head made from parian with blond painted hair style and modelled glazed cloth in light blue and pink with painted ornaments as well as beautiful hair jewelry in white and gold - painted blue eyes - closed mouth with white dividing line - cloth body with leather arms - 19 3/4in (50 cm) large - approx. 1870.

Shoulder head made from parian - blond painted hair style - modelled earrings and modelled necklace with pendant, painted blue eyes - 14 1/2in (37 cm) large - approx. 1875.

Shoulder head made from parian - black painted hair style with blue modelled hair band and blue modelled necklace with pendant - painted blue eyes - cloth body - 24 1/2in (62 cm) large - approx. 1875.

Shoulder head made from parian - blond painted hair style with blue hair band decoration - painted blue eyes - markings on the shoulder plate: 18 - 5 in (13 cm) large - approx. 1870.

  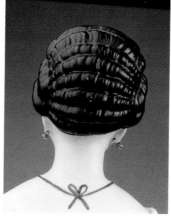 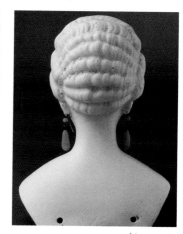

The rear of the head of the above doll.

Profile and rear of the head of the above doll.

The doll heads (Fig. upper row middle and on the right) originated - as one can see - from the same model, the doll on the right is only missing the necklace.

The rear of the head of the above doll, whose hair style is identical with the rear of the head of the doll next to it on the left.

Shoulder head made from parian - blond painted hair style - painted blue eyes - marking at the throat: 17 or 19 - cloth body with leather arms and material legs - 28 1/2in (72 cm) large - approx. 1870.

Shoulder head made from china (identical model to the picture on the left) - black painted hair style - painted eyes - cloth body - arms made from china - 19in (48 cm) large - approx. 1870.

Profile and rear of the head of the above doll.

Profile and rear of the head of the above doll.

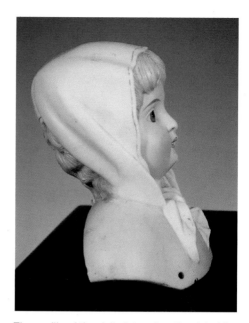

The profile of the doll pictured on the right (the back portion of the shoulder plate is missing).

Full view of the doll wearing beautiful old clothes.

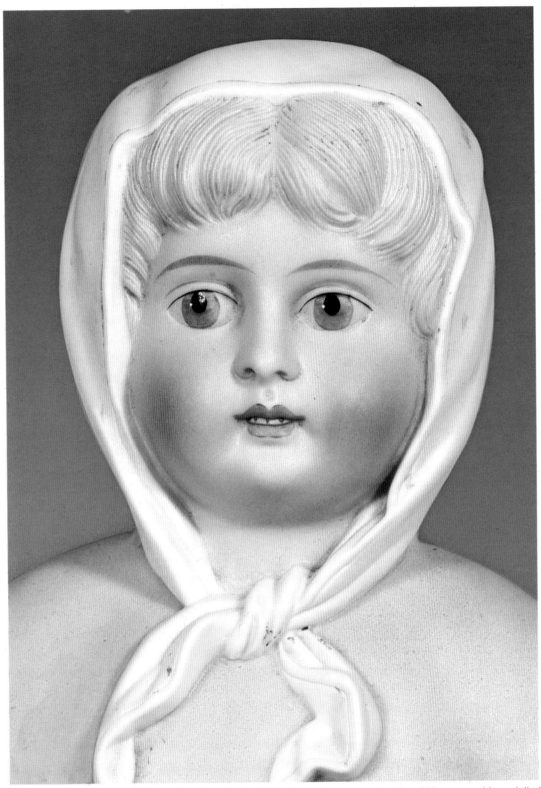

Shoulder head made from bisque - blond painted hair style - modelled shawl - painted blue eyes with modelled upper lids - open-closed mouth with contour and painted teeth (very rare) - cloth body with bisque forearms (added) - 20 1/2in (52 cm) large - approx. 1880 .

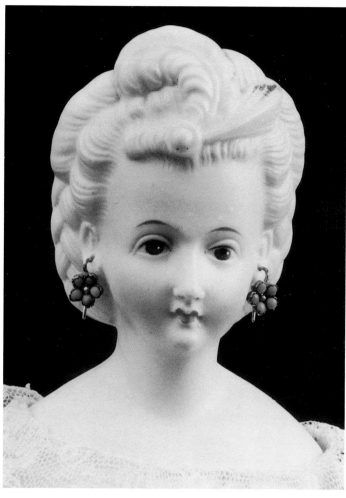 

Shoulder head made from parian - blond painted hair style with two modelled white feathers with gold at the edges - leather body - 17 1/2in (44 cm) large - approx. 1876.

Shoulder head made from bisque - blond painted hair style with gold colored hair band - marking: 14 - painted blue eyes - red cheeks - approx. 1870.

  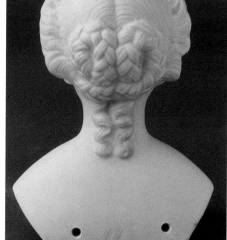

The profile of the above doll.

The rear of the head and the profile of the doll above right.

162

Shoulder head made from parian - blond painted hair style with modelled black hair band and gold colored pearls - blue glass eyes - leather body - 17 1/2in (44 cm) large - approx. 1870.

Shoulder head made from parian - blond painted hair style with modelled blue hair band and small red trimmings - painted blue eyes - 14in (36 cm) large - approx. 1870.

The profile of the doll above.

The rear of the head of the doll above.

Shoulder head made from bisque with blond painted hair style and modelled Scottish Bonnet with colored feathers, modelled blouse upper part with gold edged glazed collar as well as dotted bow - blue glass eyes - cloth body with bisque forearms and legs - 13in (33 cm) large - approx. 1885.

Swivel shoulder plate head (swivel neck) made from bisque with brown painted hair style adorned with modelled gold colored pearls - blue glass eyes - 4 3/4in (12 cm) large - approx. 1880.
The modelling and painting point to the company Dornheim, Koch & Fischer.

Shoulder head made from parian - blond painted hair style with modelled gold colored bow hair band - painted blue eyes - leather body - 24in (61 cm) large - approx. 1875.

Shoulder head made from parian - black painted hair style with the rest of a gold colored bow band - painted blue eyes - pierced ears - cloth body with china arms - 12 1/2in (32 cm) large - approx. 1875.

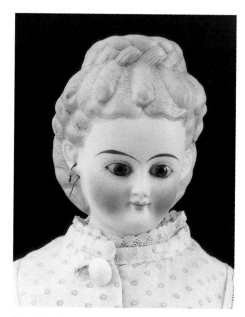

Rear of the heads of the dolls pictured above. Both dolls came from the same model - the blond doll does not have pierced ears..

Shoulder head made from parian - markings at the throat: 39 / 5 - blond painted braid hair style - blue glass eyes - leather body - 17 3/4in (45 cm) large - approx. 1875.

Rear of the head of the doll on the left.

Shoulder head made from parian - blond painted hair style with modelled rose and leaves - painted blue eyes - cloth body with china arms and legs - 15 1/2in (39 cm) large - approx. 1875 - possibly made by the company Dornheim, Koch & Fischer.

Shoulder head made from parian - markings: 10 - blond painted hair style with hair band, a pink blossom in the middle and two small pink bows at the side, modelled necklace with unpainted cross - painted eyes - leather body with leather arms and wooden legs - 23 1/2in (59 cm) large - approx. 1875.

The rear of the head of the doll above with modelled black bow.

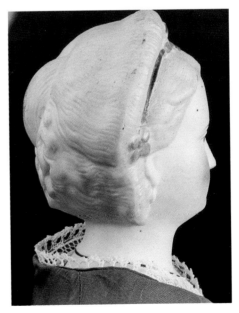

The profile of the doll above.

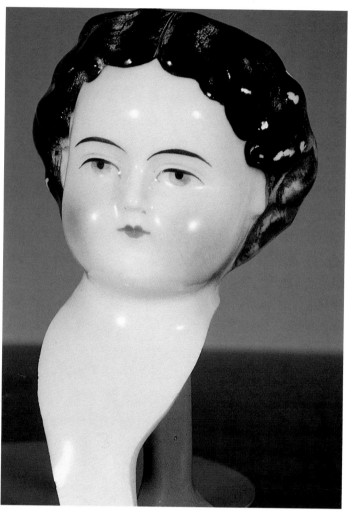
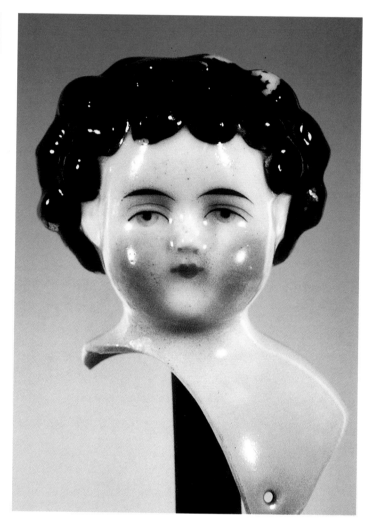

Two doll heads with broken shoulder plates, 5 1/2in (14 cm) large.

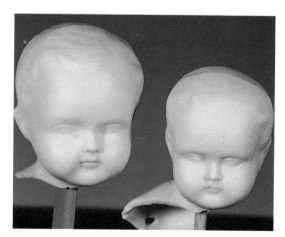

Damaged small raw models.

Damaged small raw models.

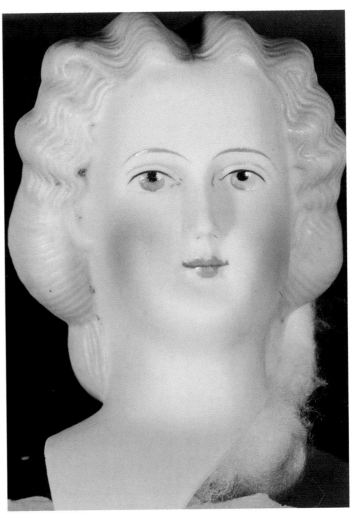

Broken middle-sized raw model, picture below left the rear of the head.

Finished painted doll head with broken shoulder plate and the picture below shows the broken rear of the head with modelled black comb.

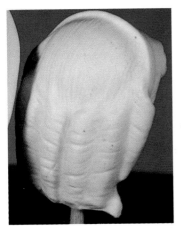

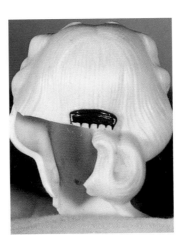

For comparison a finished painted head identical model to the one pictured above left.

All of these casts (on both pages) originated from old plaster molds, which were found in old buildings being torn down on the grounds of the company Alt, Beck & Gottschalck. The modelling of the rear of the heads in the molds were usually intentionally destroyed, so that it could not be used by any one. Worn off plaster molds were used as brick stones for buildings in the factories themselves or were sold.

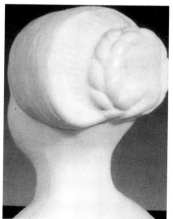

So-called Adelina Patti

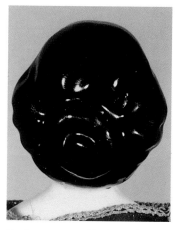

For the purpose of better understanding a finished "Jenny Lind" doll made from the period around 1870 compared with the broken rear of the head of a raw model (see Fig. middle row on the left).

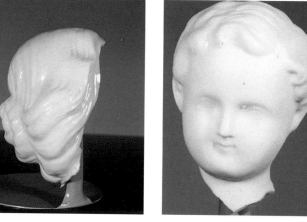

Broken rear of the head of a raw model, a Jenny-Lind doll head.

Old raw model and its rear of the head.

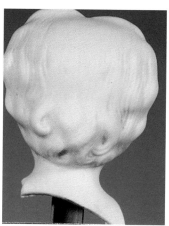

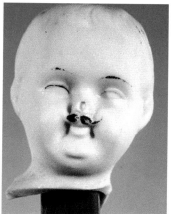

Old raw model and its rear of the head.

Old raw model.

An old doll compared with the raw model on the right- shoulder head made from bisque - blond painted hair style with modelled hair band, and necklace - glass eyes - ears pierced. Similar china heads can be found with painted eyes and black hair style.

A broken glazed raw model - 3in (8 cm) large without shoulder plate - ears pierced.

Two broken raw models of medium size.

Rear of the head of the doll pictured above.

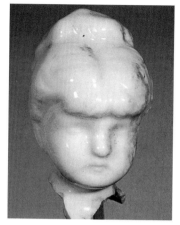
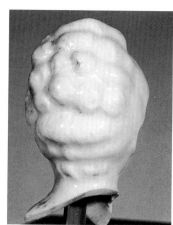

Five small broken raw models and the rear of their heads 3 - 4in (8 - 10 cm) large.

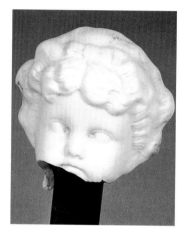

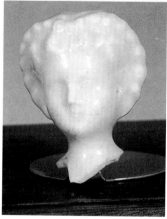
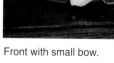

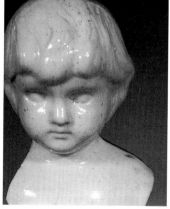
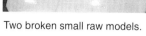

Front with small bow.

Two broken small raw models.

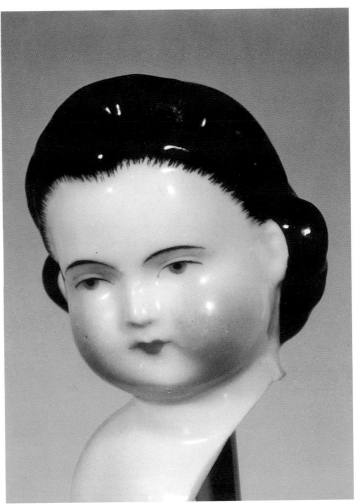

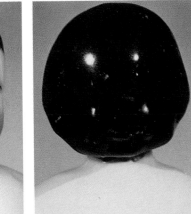

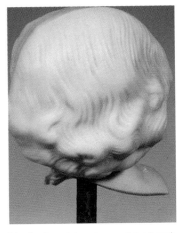

China head - 5in (13 cm) large - with broken shoulder plate ...

... - top row the smaller version of the identical model and rear of the head, as well as the identical raw model and its rear of the head.

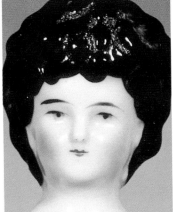

Shoulder head made from china and rear of the head with modelled black bow.

Broken glazed raw model and rear of the head with modelled bow.

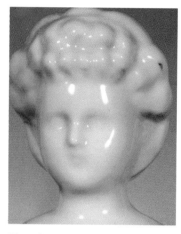   

Glazed raw model with broken shoulder plate and rear of the head with modelled bow.

Three china heads and the rear of their heads (Fig. above and middle row).

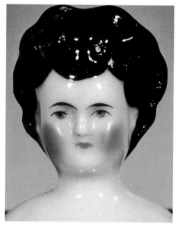 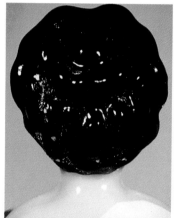  

 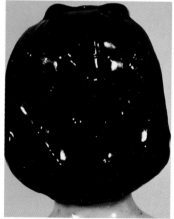  

Small shoulder head made from china with modelled hair-net and bow with bands on top of the head and rear of the head and the broken raw model of an identical model and rear of the head with hair-net and bow with bands.

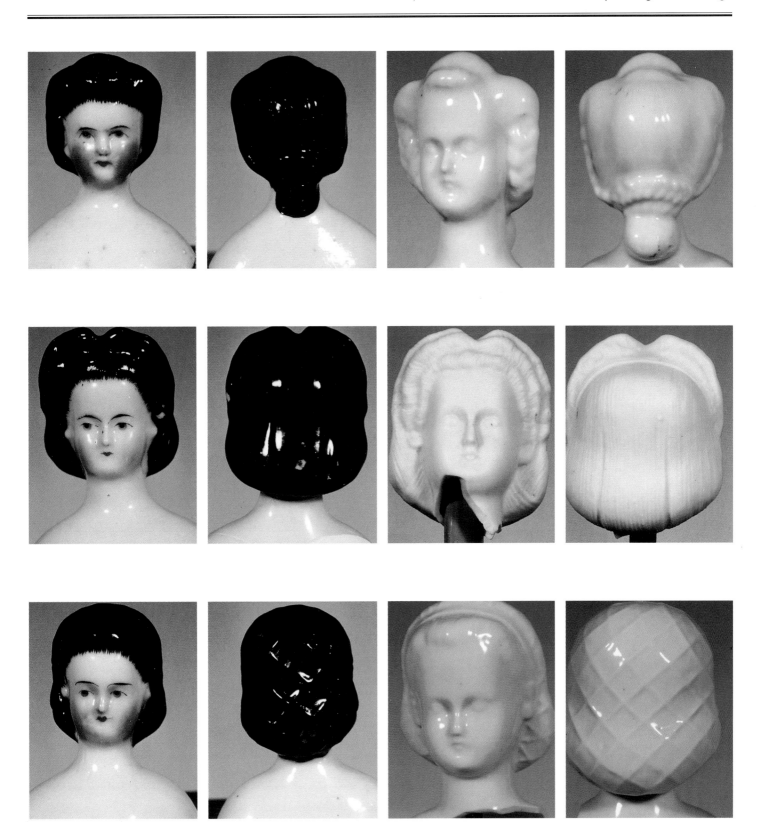

Three small shoulder heads made from china as well as their rear of the heads, respectively next to them their identical raw models and the rear of their heads.

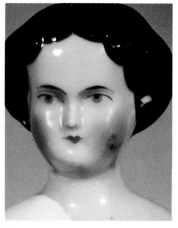 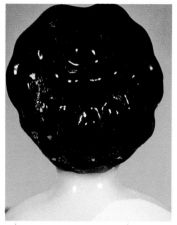  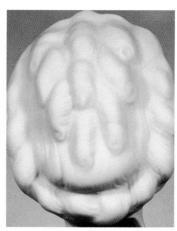

Small shoulder head made from china with rear of the head.   Broken raw model with rear of the head.

   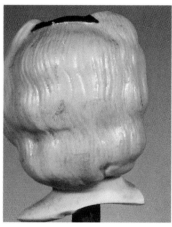

Broken raw model with rear of the head.   Broken small shoulder head made from bisque with black hair band and rear of the head.

 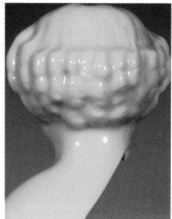  

Broken, small glazed raw model with rear of the head.   Two small broken shoulder heads made from china.

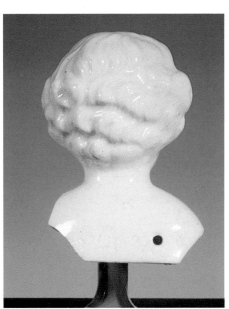

Small doll-house doll heads made from bisque, which are shown here, because the possibility exists, that identical heads were produced also in large size.

Broken glazed raw model with rear of the head.

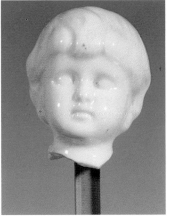

Two broken, small glazed raw models.

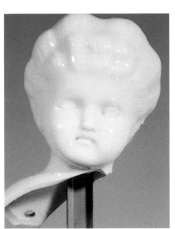

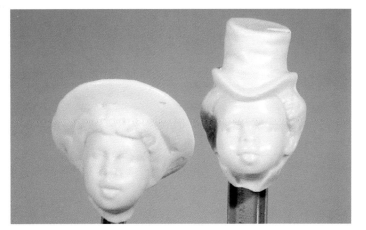

Two broken small raw models of doll heads, which may have been produced in large sizes.

The rear of the head.

Casting made from an old mold with modelled bonnet, roses on the sides.

Porcelain Factory Kleindembach

Casts made from old molds, whose rear of the heads were destroyed.

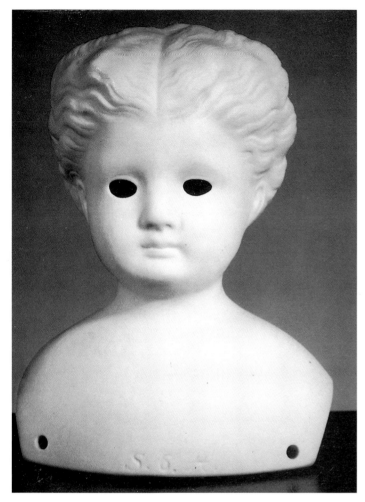

Casts made from old molds.

Type "Alice in Wonderland".

Rear of the doll heads above.

Emma Clear

Emma Clear reproduction of a "Jenny Lind" doll.

One of the largest doll experts and one who dedicated most of her life towards dolls was Emma Clear. Her name is well-known and famous in American doll collector circles. She was with body and soul a doll collector, and since she recognized, that there were not enough old dolls to provide all lovers with, she began to manufacture reproductions (replicas).

Her career began in 1888, when she started repairing dolls and producing doll clothes. In 1908 she founded the Humpty Dumpty Doll Clinic in Buffalo, New York and through her work repairing dolls, she manufactured many spare parts from porcelain dolls, acquired a large amount of knowledge as well as many skills and techniques. These skills would be used one day for producing replicas and later for dolls made after her own designs.

In 1917, she opened a Humpty Dumpty Doll Hospital in Los Angeles, and inspired from the art of doll making. Emma said that she lived to see the day, when intelligent people agreed with her opinion that the largest art of the last generation was found in expressions of dolls.

In 1939 she advertised the first American China head doll, a Jenny Lind reproduction for the price of $10. Today this doll is worth approx. $300. Emma Clear once said about her reproductions: "We do not want to imitate the old dolls, but we try, to capture their charm and beauty with the advantages of new technologies". Since they are not exactly copied, it is possible today for the skilled eye of the collector, to distinguish between an original and a reproduction.

From 1941 to 1947, Emma Clear also manufactured dolls with decorations. Her first works were unmarked, because she did not recognize the importance these dolls would hold one day. Soon after her dolls were signed on the back shoulder plate with "Clear" and quite often also with the year. Her Lady Dolls were mostly dressed with a small corset. Emma Clear gave her dolls names, which do not however always agree with the present day collector names.

Emma and her husband, who was also active in the business, worked many years without vacation, twelve hours a day and seven days a week. She maintains, that the work was her hobby and that she would be bored to death without work. Her husband invented a small body stuffer, with which he could quickly stuff the cloth bodies with sawdust. In 1949, Emma sold her business due to age and health reasons to Lillian Smith for further use.

Reproductions of old china head dolls

Today the production of replicas cannot be left out from the doll industry, because it has simply become necessary. It is a fact, that the circle of doll collectors is growing and unfortunately the number of old dolls in good condition are diminishing. A gap emerges that can only be filled by reproductions. Two demands are met: the wish for unusually rare dolls; the demand for more cheaper dolls, Thus reproductions have already taken over a firm place, though they are still considered with mistrust and fear of forgeries by some collectors. This mistrust is wrong, because reproductions are marked as a rule as such. Naturally forgeries can occur today - like in the past -, but this danger can be avoided, if one buys antique dolls only at serious dealers, through private people or at auctions.

"Good reproductions, which were still refused a couple of years ago or at the best were smiled at, are now conquering more and more the goodwill of lovers and collectors. Not only owing to the widely offered seminars and information, but the quality has clearly risen, and it can not be denied, that successful doll makers with earnest engagement have been able to give their creations something from the charm of the old models".
Christel Kesting

Those who wish to contact Christel Kesting can do so at:

Werner and Christel Kesting
Stader Straße 342a
21075 Hamburg
Germany

Bernd Ludwig, state approved porcelain modeller, and now a 20 year independent modeller, came like his grandfather and father from Thüringen, where father and grandfather had the same profession. Model and plaster mold manufacturer of character heads and artist dolls, 20 years of experience.

Bernd Ludwig
Schlesierstraße 16
96231 Staffelstein
Germany

Tel. 09573 / 6817

Reproduction of a so-called "Marguerite Doll" with butterfly bonnet.

Reproduction of a so-called "Marguerite Doll" with flower bonnet.
Both dolls were produced in the original by the company Hertwig & Co.. The reproductions were manufactured by Mrs. Christel Kesting.

Important Notes on Collecting

Many doll collectors will have this one question at heart, whether one can still collect such dolls, especially since they are so rare, and that one hardly gets to see them face to face. To say it immediately: One can and should collect them; but must be aware that it is a difficult search. Before buying one, one should take the time and patience in searching and waiting. This is the real charm of collecting. It increases the excitement and ultimately the delight in collecting, especially when one has the luck of owning a long searched for doll.

However these charming dolls are still to be found everywhere with modelled hair - even at acceptable prices -, even though not in large numbers as their younger counterparts with wigs and sleep eyes. Quite often one can find them isolated and often ignored sitting or standing around at doll fairs, in antique shops and even in flea markets, waiting for a new home, where they will be loved and valued again. Such appreciation is really needed, because they are the oldest among all china head dolls, and the thought alone, to have outlived over a hundred years.

Naturally no one must strive to find a complete collection. One doll is an enrichment and it should not be missing in a doll collection. Those collectors however, who develop with time a particular affection to them, are recommended to participate at auctions.